CELEB VIRGINS

A STORY OF THE LADIES OF LLANGOLLEN

Written by Katie Elin-Salt

Created by Katie Elin-Salt and Eleri B. Jones

FOR AMATEUR PRODUCTION ENQUIRIES

UNITED KINGDOM AND WORLD
EXCLUDING NORTH AMERICA
licensing@concordtheatricals.co.uk
020-7054-7298

Each title is subject to availability from Concord Theatricals,
depending upon country of performance.

---

and aeriplanes B.

No one shall make any changes in this title for the purpose of production. No part of this book may be reproduced, stored in a retrieval system, scanned, uploaded, or transmitted in any form, by any means, now known or yet to be invented, including mechanical, electronic, digital, photocopying, recording, videotaping, or otherwise, without the prior written permission of the publisher. No one shall share this title, or part of this title, to any social media or file hosting websites.

The moral right of Katie Elin-Salt to be identified as author of this work has been asserted in accordance with Section 77 of the Copyright, Designs and Patents Act 1988.

USE OF COPYRIGHTED MUSIC

A licence issued by Concord Theatricals to perform this play does not include permission to use the incidental music specified in this publication. In the United Kingdom: Where the place of performance is already licensed by the PERFORMING RIGHT SOCIETY (PRS) a return of the music used must be made to them. If the place of performance is not so licensed then application should be made to PRS for Music (www.prsformusic.com). A separate and additional licence from PHONOGRAPHIC PERFORMANCE LTD (www.ppluk.com) may be needed whenever commercial recordings are used. Outside the United Kingdom: Please contact the appropriate music licensing authority in your territory for the rights to any incidental music.

USE OF COPYRIGHTED THIRD-PARTY MATERIALS

Licensees are solely responsible for obtaining formal written permission from copyright owners to use copyrighted third-party materials (e.g., artworks, logos) in the performance of this play and are strongly cautioned to do so. If no such permission is obtained by the licensee, then the licensee must use only original materials that the licensee owns and controls. Licensees are solely responsible and liable for clearances of all third-party copyrighted materials, and shall indemnify the copyright owners of the play(s) and their licensing agent, Concord Theatricals Ltd., against any costs, expenses, losses and liabilities arising from the use of such copyrighted third-party materials by licensees.

IMPORTANT BILLING AND CREDIT REQUIREMENTS

If you have obtained performance rights to this title, please refer to your licensing agreement for important billing and credit requirements.

As this script went to print during rehearsals, this text may differ slightly to the original performed production.

L:

CELEBRATED VIRGINS / A STORY OF THE LADIES OF LLANGOLLEN was first produced Theatr Clwyd on 20th May 2022. The cast was as follows:

ELEANOR .... Victoria John
SARAH .... Heather Agyepong
SIR WILLIAM / WILLIAM WORDSWORTH / EDMUND BURKE
.... Seán Carlsen
LADY BETTY / MARY .... Emma Pallant

COMMUNITY CAST .... Lindsay Blessing, Pat Brewin, Liz Carter-Jones, Gwyneth Ann Dillon, Hannah Fargher, Gavin Hayes, Mair Hÿtch-Edwards, David Hÿtch, Maisie Langridge, Elliott Locke-De-Pinho, Ann Merrilees, Gerard McCann, Alison McLean, Jean Bridget Page, Lynwen Payne, Gordon Peterson, Karen Picton, Stephen Taylor

Writer – Katie Elin-Salt
Director – Eleri B. Jones
Designer – Holly Pigott
Lighting Designer – Kieron Johnson
Sound Designer – Matthew Williams
Movement Director – Jess Williams
Composer – Lynwen Haf Roberts
Casting Director – Polly Jerrold
Intimacy and Fight Director - Ruth Cooper-Brown of Rc-Annie Ltd
Dialect Coach – Natalie Grady
Assistant Director – Juliette Manon
Wellbeing Facilitator – Hester Evans
Company Stage Manager – Cassey Driver
Deputy Stage Manager – Ed Salt – Edward
Line Producer – Ric Watts
Production Manger – Jim Davis
Head of Production – Hannah Lobb
Technical Manager – Geoff Farmer
Senior Technician (Lighting) – Chris Skinner
Senior Technician (Stage) – Nic Samuel
Wardrobe Manager – Debbie Knight
Workshop Manager – Steve Eccleson
Scenic Artist – Katy Salt

CAST

(2) **VICTORIA JOHN | ELEANOR**

Victoria trained at Rose Bruford College.

Theatre credits include: *Pavilion, Wave Me Goodbye, Cyrano de Bergerac, All My Sons, The Light of Heart, Aristocrats, The Winslow Boy, Rape of the Fair Country, Boeing Boeing, Roots, The Suicide, A Chorus of Disapproval* (Theatr Clwyd); *Glitterball* (RifCo Theatre); *The Flock* (Chichester Festival Theatre); *HIR* (Bush Theatre); *Play/Silence* (The Other Room); *The Frozen Scream* (WMC/Birmingham Hippodrome); *Cancer Time* (the Caramel Club); *Never, Fear, Love?* (Velvet Ensemble/WMC); *The Gut Girls* (Velvet Ensemble/Sherman Cymru); *Treasure* (King's Head Theatre); *Reasons for Feeling* (Tristan Bates Theatre); *The Bitter Tears of Petra Von Kant* (Flaming Theatre Company) and *The Real Story of Puss in Boots* (Streetwise Fringe, Dubai).

Television: *Gwaith/Cartref* (S4C/Fiction Factory); *Miranda* (BBC); *Cast Offs* (Channel 4); Rhiannon in *Little Britain* (BBC).

Radio: *Telling the Bees* (BBC Wales).

(1) **HEATHER AGYEPONG | SARAH**

Theatre credits include: *The Body Remembers* (The Place/Fuel Theatre); *Noughts & Crosses* (Mercury Theatre Colchester/Pilot Theatre); *GIRLS* (Talawa Theatre Company/HighTide/Soho Theatre); *So Many Reasons* (Fuel Theatre/Ovalhouse Theatre) and *TYPT 16: HATCH* (Talawa Theatre Company).

Television credits include: *The Power* (Amazon Studios), *This is Going to Hurt and Enterprice* (BBC). She was nominated for the South Bank Sky Arts Breakthrough Award 2018, awarded the Firecracker Photographic Grant 2020 and was selected as part of Foam Talent 2021.

She recently won the Jerwood/Photoworks Award 2022 and The Photographers Gallery New Talent Award 2021.

Heather is a visual artist, performer/actor and maker who lives and works in London. Heather's visual art practice is concerned with mental health and wellbeing, invisibility, the diaspora and the archive.

(4) **SEÁN CARLSEN | SIR WILLIAM**

Born in South Wales, Seán trained at the Royal Welsh College of Music & Drama and has worked extensively in theatre, television and film.

Theatre credits includes: *Dust* –national tour (Quidem Productions); *Tales of the Country* (Pentabus Theatre – 2010/11 national tours); *Twelfth Night, Cymbeline* and *The Merry Wives of Windsor* (Ludlow Festival Theatre); *20,000 Leagues Under the Sea* (Watermill Theatre); *Blue Remembered Hills* (Cheltenham Everyman/Laughing Orange);

The Masque of the Red Death (Fetch Theatre); *An Enemy of the People* (Theatr Clwyd), *Sons & Lovers* (national tour); *Brief Encounter* – OTTC tour; *Rock n' Roll & Barbirolli* (Snap/Westcliff Palace Theatre); *The Picture of Dorian Gray* (national tour).

Seán has also worked with National Theatre Wales, Bristol Old Vic, Spectacle Theatre, Gwent Theatre, Theatr Powys and Theatre West Glamorgan.

TV credits includes: *His Dark Materials* (BBC); *All Creatures Great and Small* (Channel 5); *A Mother's Love* (Channel 4); *Stella* (Sky1); *Skins* (E4); *Legends* (BBC4); *Doctor Who* (BBC); *Torchwood* (BBC); *Manhunt* (ITV); *Crimewatch* (BBC); *The Great Dome Robbery* (Channel 5); *The Bench* (BBC); *Casualty* (BBC); *Tastebuddies* (BBC3); *Back Up* (BBC); *Tiger Bay* (BBC); *Mud* (CBBC); *Y Palmant Our* (S4C) and *Halen yn y Gwaed* (S4C).

Films include: *Forgotten Journeys, The Cleansing, Boudica – Rise of the Warrior Queen, Frenzy, Shine* and *Darklands*.

Seán is perhaps best known to *Doctor Who* fans as the voice of Narvin in the *Doctor Who* audio series.

③ EMMA PALLANT | LADY BETTY AND MARY

Theatre includes: *Ravens: Spassky vs Fischer* (Hampstead Theatre); *A Christmas Carol, The Dog in the Manger, Tamar's Revenge, The House of Desires, Pedro, The Great Pretender, Henry IV Parts I and II, As You Like It, Laughter in the Dark* (Royal Shakespeare Company); *Enemy of the People, LAVA* (Nottingham Playhouse); *Intra Muros* (Park Theatre); *William Wordsworth* (ETT/Theatre by the Lake); *Wind in the Willows* (Rose Theatre, Kingston); *Much Ado About Nothing, As You Like It, A Midsummer Night's Dream, Romeo and Juliet, A Comedy of Errors, Macbeth* (Shakespeare's Globe); *It Just Stopped, Alison's House* (Orange Tree); *Bell, Book and Candle, Bleak House, Great Expectations, Romeo and Juliet* (New Vic); *The Cherry Orchard, His Dark Materials, Katherine Desouza* (Birmingham Rep); *On Golden Pond, The Herbal Bed* (Salisbury Playhouse); *The House of Bernarda Alba* (Belgrade Theatre); *Cymbeline* (Regent's Park); *Top Girls* (Watford Palace); *Precious Bane* (Pentabus).

Television includes: *Father Brown, Holby City, Casualty, Doctors.*

Radio includes: *Something Understood, Messages to a Submariner, The Daughter of the Air.*

Concerts include: *WW1 Centenary: Fauré's Requiem* (Southwark Cathedral); *If This Is A Man* (Royal Festival Hall); *Shostakovich's Hamlet* (City of London Sinfonia); *Midsummer Night's Dream LPO* (Royal

Festival Hall); *A Song of Good and Evil* (Stockholm Berwaldhallen); *Shakespeare Songs* (London Jazz Festival, Sam Wanamaker Playhouse).

Emma also records audiobooks and volunteers with the children's mentoring charity, *Scene and Heard*.

CREATIVE TEAM

WRITER | KATIE ELIN-SALT

Katie is an actor/writer from Bridgend, South Wales. She first discovered a love of theatre at Bridgend Youth Theatre aged nine, and then went on to train in acting at RWCMD and worked professionally as an actor for many years – taking many roles at Theatre Clwyd such as *Educating Rita, Under Milkwood, As You Like It, Season's Greetings* and ~~most~~ *the* ~~recently~~ played Fairy Daffodil in ~~our~~ 2019 panto *Jack and The Beanstalk*. Most recently Katie has been seen on BBC Wales in *The Tuckers*.

Katie has been writing for the last five years and was mentored under the Royal Court's Introductory writers' group. She went on to secure a writing residency at Clwyd, where the idea for *Celebrated Virgins* was born. Katie worked to develop her writing voice during the pandemic and her first play *Sprinkles* was produced by Dirty Protest in December 2021. Katie has also had commissions from Sherman Theatre, Chippy Lane and is a current member of the Soho Theatre Writers' Group. In her spare time Katie is training to be a Music Therapist and enjoys working with young people as a creative engagement facilitator.

Katie is thrilled to be having her debut commissioned play premier at Theatre Clwyd, a theatre that has supported her growth from young, inexperienced actor to established company member to fully-fledged playwright over the last decade.

DIRECTOR | ELERI B. JONES

Eleri is a Welsh theatre and film director, born and raised between Llangollen and Chester. She achieved a full scholarship to the University of Manchester where she studied Drama and Screen Studies, resulting in a 1st Class Degree, before being accepted as a Leverhulme Scholar onto the MA in Screen Acting at Drama Centre, London. After seven years working as a professional actor and workshop leader, Eleri moved into directing, mentored by BAFTA winning director Carol Wiseman and was selected as one of the first two recipients of the Traineeship for Directors in Wales at Theatr Clwyd, supported by the Carne Trust and Sir Ian McKellen. Eleri's previous directing credits include the *Women Rediscovered* Film Series (written by Emyr John for Theatr Clwyd/NE Wales Archives), *Sprinkles* (written by Katie Elin-Salt for Dirty Protest), *A Christmas Carol* (devised from the original text by Eleri & Laura Marie

Donnelly for the Charles Dickens Museum) and *Gwyl Gaeaf* (written by Rebecca Wilson for the *Once Upon a Christmas* Series, Theatr Clwyd).

Eleri also works as a 1st AD, and has recently finished shooting on the Theatr Clwyd/Rondo Media production of Tim Price's *Isla* for BBC 4, directed by Tamara Harvey. The Ladies of Llangollen have been a great source of inspiration and fascination to Eleri ever since she first learned about them as a child, and she is absolutely thrilled to finally have the opportunity to bring their wonderful love story to life!

DESIGNER | HOLLY PIGOTT
Holly graduated from the Royal Welsh College of Music and Drama in 2011. She was a finalist in the Linbury Prize for Stage Design and completed a year long residency as Trainee Designer with the Royal Shakespeare Company. Holly designs for both stage and screen, her recent credits including; Assistant Costume Designer on *The Confessions of Frannie Langton* (ITV / Drama Republic) and Set and Costume Designer for *The Picture of Dorian Gray, The Importance of Being Ernest* and *Going the Distance* – all digital productions for Lawrence Batley Theatre. Other credits include: *Fleabag* (Wyndham's Theatre); *Ages Of The Moon* (Vaults Theatre); *The Talented Mr Ripley* (Stephen Joseph Theatre, Northern Stage + Lawrence Batley Theatre); *Sex With A Stranger* (Trafalgar Studios); *La Scala Di Seta* (Linbury Studio, Royal Opera House); *International Opera Awards* 2017, 2018 and 2019 (London Coliseum & Sadler's Wells); *The Island* (Young Vic); *The Prophet* (Gate Theatre); *Partenope* and *L'elisir d'amore* (Iford Opera); *The Magic Flute* (Copenhagen Opera Festival), *The Turn Of The Screw, Mad King Suibhne* and *Aurora* (Bury Court Opera); *Little Wolf* (Chapter Arts Centre); *Constellations* (Theatre Municipal De Fontainebleau); *Skin A Cat* (Bunker Theatre, Edinburgh Fringe and UK Tour); *Elegy For A Lady* and *The Yalta Game* (Salisbury Playhouse); *Klippies, Beast* and *East of Berlin* (Southwark Playhouse); *Caterpillar* (Theatre 503); *Lean* (Tristan Bates); *Eight Songs For A Mad King, Now This Is Not The End* and *Handel Furioso* (Arcola); *The Moor* (Old Red Lion); *Die Fledermaus* (OperaUpClose).

LIGHTING DESIGNER | KIERON JOHNSON
Kieron is a lighting designer for Theatre, Opera and Dance. Kieron has worked with many world renowned institutions such as Trinity Laban, London Contemporary Dance School and the Northern School of Contemporary Dance.

Recent credits include *As You Like It* (Northern Broadsides); *West Side Story: Symphonic Dances* (Opera North); *Decades: Stories from the City* (Leeds Playhouse); *Black Waters* & *EBÓ* (Phoenix Dance Theatre); *Head Above Water* and *Tides* (Joss Arnott Dance).

SOUND DESIGNER | MATTHEW WILLIAMS

Matthew, known to everyone as Wills, trained at Theatr Clwyd and The School of Sound Recording, Manchester. Wills has designed sound for around ninety productions at Theatr Clwyd over his thirty years in the building.

Wills is an award-nominated sound designer and has had his sound designs as part of exhibitions all over the world, including the V&A Museum, London. As well as theatre sound design, Wills also works with a number of bands, in both video and audio and also designed soundscapes for three escape rooms. He has an audio services company called, WW Audio, and co owns the Elsberdance dance school with his choreographer partner, Rachel.

MOVEMENT DIRECTOR | JESS WILLIAMS

Jess works as a Movement Director, Director and Performer for Theatre and VR. She trained at the London Contemporary Dance School and the Laban Centre.

Jess is Creative Associate of ThickSkin, based in Manchester. Most recently she Co-created and Directed *Sorry, I Disappeared* a walking audio play and *Petrichor* a Theatre in VR experience for ThickSkin and has a number of projects in development with them.

Jess has been a practitioner for Frantic Assembly since 2012 and was Associate Director of *I Think We Are Alone* and *The Unreturning*. She toured the UK in *The Curious Incident of the Dog in the Night-Time* for the National Theatre and Frantic Assembly and has been Associate Movement Director for the USA, World Tour, UK Tour and West End productions of the same show.

Other recent credits include: *The Boy with Two Hearts* (Wales Millennium centre); *Beginning* (National theatre, Queens theatre Hornchurch); *The Ocean at the End of the Lane* (The National Theatre); *Ignition* (Frantic Assembly); *A Walk is Not a Walk* (Lyric Belfast); *One flew over the Cuckoo's Nest* (English Theatre Frankfurt); *Constellations* (National Centre for Performing Arts, Mumbai); *Merched Caerdydd* (Theatr Genedlaethol Cymru); *Tuck* and *A Good Clean Heart* (Wales Millennium Centre); *Wonderland* (Nottingham Playhouse).

COMPOSER | LYNWEN HAF ROBERTS

Lynwen is an emerging Composer and Musical Director currently based in Mold. Her recent commissions include *Barry Harden – Facebook Troll!* (Academi Leeway/Leeway Productions) and *Golygfeydd o'r Pla Du* (Theatrau Sir Gâr & Chris Harris). She is also a participant of the inaugural MD Mentorship Scheme 2021-22, and has been assigned as a mentee to London MD Mark Collins, partaking in regular skill sharing sessions as well as shadowing him in the orchestra pits of current West End shows.

Lynwen is also an experienced actor-musician, and has over ten years of experience working in Theatre, TV and Radio here in Wales and across the UK. Recent credits include: *Summer Holiday, Blonde Bombshells of 1943, The Crucible* (Pitlochry Festival Theatre); *Clera* (Arad Goch); *Pobol y Cwm* (BBC) and *The News From Nowhere* (BBC Radio 4). She has also appeared in Theatr Clwyd's infamous Rock 'n' Roll pantos for the last five years; *Beauty and the Beast, The Panto that Nearly Never Was!, Jack and the Beanstalk, Dick Whittington* and *Sleeping Beauty*.

CASTING DIRECTOR | POLLY JERROLD
Polly previously worked as the Casting Associate at the Royal Exchange Theatre for five years.

Theatre credits include: *Antigone* (Regent's Park Open Air Theatre); *Chasing Hares, The Secretaries* (Young Vic Theatre); *First Touch* (Nottingham Playhouse); *Life of Pi* (Sheffield Theatres & West End); *Waldo's* (Extraordinary Bodies/Bristol Old Vic); *Pretty Shitty Love, Celebrated Virgins, Curtain Up* and *For the grace of you go I* (Theatr Clwyd); *Shandyland* (Northern Stage); *One Flew Over the Cuckoo's Nest, Tribes* (Sheffield Theatres); *Our Lady of Kibeho, Soul, Merlin, Peter And The Starcatcher* (Royal & Derngate); *Two Trains Running* (ETT and Royal & Derngate); *Approaching Empty* (Kiln, Tamasha & Live Theatre); *The Lovely Bones* (Royal & Derngate, Birmingham Rep and Northern Stage); *To Kill A Mockingbird, Running Wild* (Regent's Park tour); *Peter Pan, A Tale of Two Cities, Oliver Twist,* (Regent's Park Open Air Theatre); *All's Well that Ends Well* (Shakespeare's Globe); *The Caretaker* (Bristol Old Vic); *The Government Inspector, Tommy, Our Country's Good* (Ramps on the Moon); *The Island Nation* (Arcola); *Brideshead Revisited, A View from the Bridge, Sherlock* (York Theatre Royal); *Anita & Me, Peter Pan, Of Mice and Men, A Christmas Carol, 101 Dalmatians, What Shadows, Folk, Winnie And Wilbur, Back Down, Feed the Beast, I Knew You* (Birmingham Rep); *The Kitchen Sink, Educating Rita* (Hull Truck Theatre); *Sweet Charity, Wit, The Ghost Train* and *Little Shop of Horrors* (Royal Exchange Theatre).

INTIMACY AND FLIGHT DIRECTOR | RUTH COOPER-BROWN OF RC-ANNIE LTD
RC-ANNIE Ltd, established in 2005 by Rachel Bown-Williams and Ruth Cooper-Brown, is the UK's leading Dramatic Violence and Intimacy Company.

Theatr Clwyd credits include: *Beauty and the Beast, Orpheus Descending, The Rise and Fall of Little Voice, Uncle Vanya, Jumpy, My People, All My Sons, Aristocrats.* Other credits include: *Richard III, Henry VI: Rebellion, The Wars of* the Roses Henry VI Part 1 Rehearsal Room Project, King John, Measure for Measure, As You Like It, The Taming of the Shrew, Tartuffe, The Duchess of Malfi, Salome & Snow in Midsummer (Royal Shakespeare Company); Henry VIII, Julius Caesar, Romeo and Juliet, Playing Shakespeare with Deutsche Bank – Macbeth, Macbeth, Emilia, Othello, The Secret Theatre, Boudica, Lions and Tigers, Much Ado About Nothing, Twelfth Night, Comus and Imogen (Shakespeare's Globe); As You Like It (Globe on Tour); The Scandal at Mayerling (Scottish Ballet); Theodora (Royal Opera House); The Father and the Assassin, The Welkin, Three Sisters, Anna, When We Have Sufficiently Tortured Each Other, Common, Ugly Lies the Bone, Peter Pan, The Threepenny Opera, The James Plays (co-production with National Theatre of Scotland and Edinburgh International Festival) and Cleansed (National Theatre); Persuasion (Rose Theatre Kingston); 2:22 A Ghost Story (West End); The Play What I Wrote (Birmingham Rep & Tour); The Life of Pi (Wyndham Theatre); Blue/Orange (Theatre Royal Bath); Beauty and the Beast (Theatr Clwyd); Night Mother (Hampstead Theatre); East is East (Birmingham Rep/National Theatre/Chichester Festival Theatre); Once Upon A Time in Nazi Occupied Tunisia (Almeida Theatre); The Prince of Egypt (Dreamworks at The Dominion Theatre); A Monster Calls (Old Vic Productions National Tour); Alone in Berlin (Royal and Derngate); [BLANK] (Donmar Warehouse); Macbeth (Chichester Festival Theatre); Hedda Tesman (Headlong/Chichester Festival Theatre/The Lowry); The King of Hell's Palace (Hampstead Theatre); Peter Pan (National Theatre); Troubadour (White City Theatre); Noises Off (Lyric Hammersmith & West End); The Night of the Iguana (Noel Coward Theatre); Plenty (Chichester Festival Theatre); Hobson's Choice (Manchester Royal Exchange); King Hedley (Theatre Royal Stratford East); The Little Matchgirl; (Bristol Old Vic / Shakespeare's Globe); A Very, Very, Very Dark Matter (The Bridge Theatre); Wise Children (Wise Children & The Old Vic); Company (Elliot Harper Productions at The Gielgud Theatre); Europe (Leeds Playhouse); God of Carnage, The Price, Switzerland & Dusty (Theatre Royal Bath); A Monster Calls, Woyzeck (Old Vic).

DIALECT COACH | NATALIE GRADY

TV and Film includes: Better (BBC); Happy Valley (BBC); The Reckoning (BBC); The Gallows Pole (BBC); The Birth Of Daniel F Harris (C4); Red Rose (BBC/Netflix); Rule Of The Game (BBC); Anne (ITV); Jingle Bell Christmas (Hallmark); Wolfe (SKY), Stephen (ITV), The Iprcress File (ITV); Time (BBC); Ackley Bridge (Channel 4); All Creatures Great and Small (C5 and PBS for the US); The Cure (Chanelle 4); Trip (Channel 4); Gwen (Feature Film for Endor productions); Your Christmas Or Mine (Feature Film).

credits

Theatre includes: *Nora, Gee and Met, Wuthering Heights, Gypsy, Light Falls, West Side Story, Queens of the coal age* (Royal Exchange); *Hangmen* (Golden Theatre Broadway); *Hull and High Water, A Short History of Tractors in Ukrainian, The Last Testament of Lililian Bilocca* (Hull Truck); *The Nicol Project (MIF)*; *Scoring a Century* (British Youth Oppera); *Lancastrians* (Junction 8); *Jess and Joe Forever* (Stephen Joseph Theatr); *Chicken Soup* (Sheffield Crucible); *Bread and Roses, Jumpers for Goalposts, Brassed Off* (Oldham Coliseum); *Beggars Opera, Little Shop of Horrors, Blue Stockings, Wizard of Oz* (Storyhouse); *Hoard Festival, Seeing The Lights, Beryl* (New Vic Theatre); *La Vie Parisienne, Street Scene* (RNCM); *The Last Yankee, A View From The Bridge, Two, Two 2* (Octagon Theatre); *To Kill A Mockingbird* (UK tour and Barbican).

ASSISTANT DIRECTOR | JULIETTE MANON

Juliette is a Queer Welsh/French Director, Playwright and Theatre-Maker from Mold (North Wales). They're passionate about creating work that amplifies LGBTQ+ voices, women and nonbinary people's voices and any other voice that is currently under-represented (or rather, not represented) on the Welsh stage and screen. They're a member of the Sherman Theatre's 'Unheard Voices' Writer's Group and Theatr Genedlaethol's 'Young Playwright Programme' (2021-23). Their current projects include being co-Artistic Director of their new theatre company: Cwmni Cwiar and developing their play *Bébé Gay*. Their credits include work with Theatr Clwyd, Wales Millennium Centre, National Youth Theatre of Wales, Solomonic Peacocks Theatre, Frân Wen Young Company, The Sherman Theatre, Theatr Genedlaethol Cymru, Channel 4, BBC and S4C.

Theatr Clwyd

The award-winning Theatr Clwyd is Wales' biggest producing theatre. Since 1976 Theatr Clwyd has created exceptional theatre from its home in Flintshire, North Wales. Driven by the vision and dynamism of award-winning Artistic Director Tamara Harvey and Executive Director Liam Evans-Ford, Theatr Clwyd pushes theatrical boundaries creating world-class productions.

In 2021 Theatr Clwyd was named as The Stage's *Regional Theatre Of The Year*. Major recent successes have included co-producing *Home, I'm Darling* with the National Theatre, which won Best New Comedy at the Olivier Awards and was nominated in five categories, the UK Theatre Award-winning musical *The Assassination of Katie Hopkins*, the site-specific, immersive *Great Gatsby*, Menier Chocolate Factory co-production of *Orpheus Descending* and the world premiere of musical, *Milky Peaks*.

Theatr Clwyd is one of only four theatres in the UK to build sets and props, make costumes and paint scenery in-house. Their impressive team of workshop, wardrobe and scenic artists, props makers and technicians ensure the skills vital to a vibrant theatre industry are nurtured right in the heart of Wales, developing the theatre makers of the future. In addition to this, Theatr Clwyd hosts an artist development programme, trainee technicians' scheme and an eighteen-month traineeship for directors, to develop the Artistic Directors of the future.

Theatr Clwyd works in the community across all art forms and is recognised as a cultural leader for its cross generational theatre groups, work in youth justice and diverse programme of arts, health and wellbeing. Award-winning Community Engagement projects include *Arts from the Armchair*, in partnership with Betsi Cadwaladr University Health Board, which uses theatrical making skills to help people with early onset memory loss and their carers, and *Justice In A Day*, working in schools and the law courts to help at risk children to realise the consequences of crime.

Theatr Clwyd has completed the public consultation period for a major Capital Redevelopment Project which will reimagine the theatre's public spaces and create a greener, more efficient and sustainable building where world-class art can thrive and social action is rooted for generations to come.

During the Covid-19 pandemic the theatre has been active in helping its community, from hosting blood donation sessions and distributing food to vulnerable families to creating digital dance workshops for those with Parkinsons and sharing creative packages and activities with those most isolated.

THANK YOU

Thank you to all the teams at Theatr Clwyd

Thank you to all the funders and supporters of Theatr Clwyd

The Carne Trust has been instrumental in creating the Theatr Clwyd Carne Traineeship for Directors in Wales. Eleri B. Jones, director of *Celebrated Virgins*, was one of the first two participants of the scheme.

ACKNOWLEDGEMENTS

Thank you to everyone involved in the creation and making of this show. So many people supported us throughout its development, without whom this show would not be what it is. Particular thanks to Tamara Harvey, Liam Evans-Ford, Elizabeth Mavor, The O'Connor family, John Kirwan, Parks Section of Kilkenny County Council and Woodstock Estate, Paul Evans and Plas Newydd Llangollen, "The Lesbian Commune" – Helen Holmes, Em Fitzgerald and Angel Houghton-Knapp, Juliette Manon, Maisie Langdridge, Maddie O'Dwyer, Polly Jerrold, Rebecca Jade Hammond, Victoria John, Isaura Barbé-Brown, Annette Flynn, Gareth Cassidy, Raphael Martin, Claire Salt, Joy Allen, David Salt, Pete Mooney, Emily Joy Salt, Spencer Peach, James Salt, Sam Jones, Heather Richards, Mike Murray, Issy Richards, Gladstone's Library, Nick Gauntlett, Charlotte Morgan Jones, Morgan Lloyd-Malcom, Tim Price, Alexa Morden, Alice Kickham, Jess Legg, Joel Horwood and Maria Aberg.

Gypsy wood, Charlie Quinn,
Sinead O'Connor

CHARACTERS

SARAH
ELEANOR
LADY BETTY / MARY CARYLL
SIR WILLIAM / WILLIAM WORDSWORTH / EDMUND BURKE

All other roles can be split amongst the cast or used as voices.

The community cast/witness roles should be played by members of the community in which this play is being performed.

LOCATION

The first half of this story takes place in Kilkenny, Ireland.
The second half takes place in Llangollen, Wales.

AUTHOR'S NOTES

Although this story is inspired by true events, it is a reimagining viewed through a modern-day lens and not a historically accurate re-enactment. With this in mind, I would encourage any future productions to make bold creative choices that not only reflect the period in which this play is set – but ones that also celebrate the diversity of the world around us today.

A note on time

This play primarily follows the life of Sarah Ponsonby from age nine to her death aged seventy eight. In our world, time is fluid and dreamlike as Sarah revists snapshots of her life and re-lives them as if for the first time. All other characters exist within Sarah's memory, but wholly and truthfully within their own circumstances and time.

Music

I was listening to a lot of Sinead O'Connor whilst writing this play. All of it is relevant but specifically the songs *Mandinka*, *All Apologies* and *In This Heart*.

"There is indeed no other refuge from the horrors of history but in the mild majesty of private life"
– Mrs Elizabeth Carter (letter to Miss Catherine Talbot)

"A day of most sweetly enjoyed retirement. A day according to our hearts. Silent. Undisturbed"
– Lady Eleanor Butler's diary

ACT ONE

Scene One

A Theatre

(The initial state should have the quality of the beginnings of a dream.)

(As the audience enters, members of a community cast weave in and out of the set. They should have the feel of ghosts being conjured from the past. They should be dressed in working-class clothes from the period of the 1700s. They either don't speak at all, or if voices are heard, they are faded and unclear. Eventually, most of the ghosts fade away – although one or two remain throughout to bear witness to the story. A representation of the eyes of the period and the constant gaze of the community – always present, always somehow a part of the story. They are faceless now and their names are forgotten, but they are never to be dismissed or forgotten entirely.)

*(**SARAH** enters through the audience. A woman in her mid-late 30s. She is dressed in dishevelled upper-class men's clothes of the period in which she lived. She should look really cool and powerful, a visual*

1

representation of the image she would like to present to us today.)

(She stands centre stage, and smiles at the audience.)

(Waits for absolute silence.)

SARAH. Are you listening now?

Took you a while there, didn't it?

But maybe you didn't know if I was...

Didn't expect me to be...

Thought I might be...

Well anyway, I'm not...that.

I'm this.

Here.

Now.

Who were you expecting?

You know me.

Don't you?!

(She looks round at the audience.)

No?

Interesting.

(Beat.)

You do know I'm dead, don't you?

Really dead.

Seriously dead.

In fact I could have lived this life you are here for nearly three times over in the time it's taken you to ask me anything about it.

And you don't seem to need my help at all.

Look.

My name is written on the pages in front of you.

My face is hanging up in the National Portrait Gallery.

Tourists come over to take photos with my bones.

My home... property of the local council, there's a guided tour round there twice a day now, a really rather reasonable rate out of season.

My life... poured out in ink over the desks of long dead men.

My sex... well I imagine you suspect a bit about that of course.

Why else would you have bought a ticket?

> *(Beat.)*

Unless...

> *(Beat.)*

> *(She smiles.)*

Ah, of course.

My love.

My love, my love, my love.

You're here for her.

Still can't quite get your hands on that one, can you?

All these years...

All this time.

She is still quite my own.

Dead.

Buried.

Safe underneath me.

Delicious seclusion.

Do you understand how it works yet?

>   *(Beat.)*

Now?!

>   (**LADY BETTY** *enters, with maids.)*

LADY BETTY. Sarah, we don't have time for this.

>   *(She circles around* **SARAH.***)*

Let's have a look at you.

I'm sorry I couldn't come sooner.

Speak up!

All will be well, Sarah.

Don't keep everyone waiting.

>   *(The maids edge closer to* **SARAH** *and as they do she screams at them.)*

SARAH. I'LL NOT GO!

>   *(The maids restrain* **SARAH.***)*

>   *(They dress her in a more young ladylike fashion.)*

>   *(She is taken down into her past.)*

Scene Two

Sarah's First Home – Kilkenny, Ireland

(**SARAH** *is fighting with the maids.*)

(*The Maid attempts to lift* **SARAH.**)

(*She is a dead weight.*)

(**SIR WILLIAM** *enters.*)

SIR WILLIAM. Not as we expected, is she?

LADY BETTY. My Lord, I can only apologise.

(**SIR WILLIAM** *approaches* **SARAH.**)

SIR WILLIAM. Hello there young Madam!

Hello?

(**SARAH** *hisses at him like a feral cat.*)

(**SIR WILLIAM** *makes to leave.*)

Well, that's that then.

LADY BETTY. We can't just leave her.

SIR WILLIAM. Why not?

LADY BETTY. We made an arrangement.

SIR WILLIAM. Send word, tell them she's faulty.

LADY BETTY. She has nowhere else to go!

(**LADY BETTY** *goes to her, puts her hand on her.*)

Sarah.

Sarah.

Sarah, please.

> (**SARAH** *takes off her shoe and flings it at*
> **LADY BETTY**.*)*

> *(She tries to run away but the maids block
> her exit.)*

> *(They stand guard, ready to take her out
> again if she steps out of line.)*

Sarah.

Enough of this.

Your Father is dead.

Your stepmother does not want you here any longer.

You are to come with myself and Sir William today, and
that is the way of it.

> (**SARAH** *looks around for a friend but she
> can't find one.)*

There is nowhere else for you to go.

> *(Eventually she begrudgingly puts her shoes
> back on.)*

Good girl.

Come now.

Don't keep everyone waiting.

> (**LADY BETTY** *and* **SIR WILLIAM** *exit along with
> the maids.)*

> (**SARAH** *tries to speak to the audience and
> finds she can't.)*

> (**SARAH** *travels to Woodstock.)*

(**SARAH** *is isolated and ignored in a big house, lots of people passing by working, nobody noticing her.*)

(*In the end,* **SARAH** *sits in the middle of the stage, alone.*)

Scene Three

Woodstock, Kilkenny

(**LADY BETTY** *enters.*)

LADY BETTY. Ah, there you are.

(**SARAH** *looks up, startled.*)

LADY BETTY. Not trying to run away from me there, are you?

SARAH. No, I was just/

LADY BETTY. It's alright.

Nicer outside anyway.

(**LADY BETTY** *sits with* **SARAH.**)

Did you have a garden in your old house?

SARAH. Yes, my Father built it.

LADY BETTY. Is that so?

SARAH. I helped him sometimes.

LADY BETTY. Were you any good at it?

SARAH. Well, I can't dig very fast but I'm very good at planting seeds.

LADY BETTY. Are you now?

Perhaps we could have a word with Master Jacob, see if he'd like a small hand out here.

Would you like that ?

(**SARAH** *nods.*)

SARAH. We'll have a look into that then.

Now, shall we give this another little try?

(**LADY BETTY** *produces a cross stitch.*)

(*She passes it to* **SARAH**.)

(**SARAH** *fumbles with it then throws it away.*)

SARAH. I can't do it!

LADY BETTY. Here, look, give it to me.

(**LADY BETTY** *threads the needle back and fixes the stitch, then gives it back to* **SARAH**. **SARAH** *slowly begins to stitch, quietly.* **LADY BETTY** *watches her.*)

That's better now, isn't it?

(*Beat.*)

There's no rush, you know.

You can take your time here.

We've plenty of it.

I'm just happy you're here at all.

(**SIR WILLIAM** *enters, and speaks loudly, startling* **SARAH**.)

SIR WILLIAM. Good day Miss Sarah, are you well

(**SARAH** *jumps up and runs to hide.*)

SIR WILLIAM. Never says a word to anyone.

Just sits around the garden like a sad little gnome.

LADY BETTY. She's still settling.

SIR WILLIAM. I feel like a beast stalking the walls of my own home.

LADY BETTY. Give her time.

SIR WILLIAM. Six months Lady Betty!

Enough of it.

I want her out by the end of the week.

LADY BETTY. That's impossible.

SIR WILLIAM. How can it be impossible when she has no business being here in the first place?

LADY BETTY. She is our ward of care.

SIR WILLIAM. What does that even mean?

Tell me Lady Betty, why exactly was it that we agreed to this?

(Beat.)

Go on.

LADY BETTY. I thought it might be nice for you to have a young companion.

SIR WILLIAM. Worked out well, hasn't it?

(Beat.)

How long must I be punished for your shortcomings as a wife.

LADY BETTY. What do you mean?

SIR WILLIAM. Stealing the first available orphan.

Pretty desperate measures, don't you think?

(Beat.)

(A blue flower grows through the stage.)

*(**SARAH** spots it.)*

(She goes to it, plucks it out.)

(Studies it.)

SARAH. Bachelor's button.

LADY BETTY. What?

SARAH. Bachelor's button.

Centaurea cynus.

Cornflower.

LADY BETTY. Where did you learn that?

SARAH. My father taught me.

(They both watch her looking at the flower.)

LADY BETTY. You like it out here, don't you Sarah?

(SARAH nods.)

Give Sir William the flower.

(SARAH hesitates.)

He has been very kind to you,

Letting you share his garden.

Do you not think so?

(She gives the flower to SIR WILLIAM and curtseys.)

(He stares at it.)

SIR WILLIAM. Bachelor's Button.

Why is that?

(Beat.)

SARAH. Gentlemen wear them in their button holes when they are in love, and when the flower blooms they can be married.

SIR WILLIAM. Is that so?

LADY BETTY. She's a keen interest in gardening.

Perhaps Sarah might like to join you on your evening round Sir William.

She's never been any further than the lawn.

What do you think?

SIR WILLIAM. I'm not sure that would be/

LADY BETTY. Sarah... would you like to see the orangery?

(**SARAH** *nods.*)

Well now, there we are. Sir William?

SIR WILLIAM. We could give it a try, I suppose.

LADY BETTY. Wonderful idea.

Sounds like a lovely evening for you both all together.

I shall tell the kitchen to expect you together.

Enjoy the grounds, Sarah.

(**LADY BETTY** *exits.*)

(*Silence.*)

SIR WILLIAM. Now then.

Would you perhaps have any interest in seeing a real life lemon?

(**SARAH** *looks up at* **SIR WILLIAM** *and nods.*)

Shall we?

(*He offers his hand to* **SARAH**, *which she takes.*)

(*Together they walk the garden,* **SARAH** *planting seeds and watching some of them grow.*)

(*The flowers are not colourful yet.*)

Scene Four

Woodstock, Kilkenny

*(**LADY BETTY** enters and the two of them plant flowers all around her.)*

*(They play together, **LADY BETTY** watching them, bemusedly laughing.)*

LADY BETTY. Sir William, would you kindly desist in this distraction!

SIR WILLIAM. Oh forgive us Lady Betty, we are in chronic good humour. We have spent the day accompanying Master Jacob on gardening duties.

Sarah was most enthralled.

SARAH. We planted sprouts!

LADY BETTY. Did you now?

SARAH. Alongside Master Jacob, watered all the seeds.

SIR WILLIAM. Tell Lady Betty the ground plans of the season, Sarah.

SARAH. Now...

(She surveys the stage as if it were a garden.)

Along the terrace there will be Hemerocallis fulva, Rhododendron macrophyllum and Viola wittrockiana – these shall bloom in the summer if we keep the soil moist and the cats distracted.

On the cross path we have placed the Taxus baccata and Prunus spinosa, though of course we won't see those till the Autumn.

And finally along the side banks we harvested Citrus sinensis.

Guess what those are?

Go on?

LADY BETTY. You'll have to enlighten me.

SARAH. MASSIVE ORANGES!

> (**SARAH** *pulls an orange out of her dress and hands one to* **SIR WILLIAM** *and one to* **LADY BETTY**.)

LADY BETTY. Very good Sarah.

SIR WILLIAM. Most well versed in the latin vernacular of all your little plants and such.

SARAH. I have studied them.

SIR WILLIAM. Isn't she a clever girl?

LADY BETTY. Indeed.

> (*Beat.*)

There has been talk of your gardening interests throughout the staff.

SARAH. Really?

LADY BETTY. Wandering about the walled gardens in your day dress, reading verse after verse amongst the yews. Quite the vision, it seems.

Master Jacob doesn't know at all where to put himself, I am told.

> (**SIR WILLIAM** *laughs.*)

SIR WILLIAM. Do you blush Sarah?

SARAH. No.

SIR WILLIAM. Your cheeks are flushed.

SARAH. I have been running, Sir.

SIR WILLIAM. There is no need to feel shy.

You are much loved here, by all of us.

Two years here, blooming like the narcissus each spring.

    (Beat.)

Whatever shall become of you in summertime, I wonder?

LADY BETTY. My Lord, I thought it may be time to discuss the boarding house.

SIR WILLIAM. Bit soon, isn't it?

LADY BETTY. I don't think so.

I was thirteen when I first attended.

And she will be well looked after.

SIR WILLIAM. By whom?

LADY BETTY. Lady Butler writes to me, her own daughter has just been taken on as an aide there.

Lady Eleanor Butler.

SIR WILLIAM. Of Kilkenny castle?

LADY BETTY. The very same.

SIR WILLIAM. What is she doing working in the boarding house?

LADY BETTY. Her family seem quite at a loss as to what else to do with her, I am told.

SIR WILLIAM. Oh well, they should get on well then.

LADY BETTY. So we are in agreement then Sir?

SIR WILLIAM. Lady Betty, I'm not sure I quite understand the cause of this sudden action.

LADY BETTY. It's not sudden my Lord, it was your idea.

SIR WILLIAM. Was it?

LADY BETTY. Yes, you spoke at great lengths the other evening of the importance in broadening the minds of the young.

SIR WILLIAM. I have no recollection of saying such.

LADY BETTY. An enthralling conversation led by yourself, over dinner with Lord and Lady Tighe – most forward thinking.

They were terribly impressed.

> (**SIR WILLIAM** *is confused.*)

SIR WILLIAM. Ah, yes. Now I am remembered. I do forget the impression I make upon others with my simple musings.

LADY BETTY. She's a keen interest in learning.

Much better than sitting about the garden in the dirt reading musty old books, do you not think?

SIR WILLIAM. I suppose a small education can do a young woman no permanent damage.

LADY BETTY. Very good so.

I shall draft a letter to Miss Parkes and inform her of Sarah's desire to study.

SARAH. But I/

LADY BETTY. All will be well Sarah.

> (**LADY BETTY** ~~exists.~~) exits

SIR WILLIAM. You shall of course be expected to come back and visit us in all holidays and breaks, yes?

> (**SARAH** *looks at him for a while, then just nods.*)

Good girl.

I fear we should all go quite mad without you.

(**SIR WILLIAM** *exits.*)

(**SARAH** *is alone again.*)

Scene Five

Miss Parkes School for Girls, Kilkenny

*(**SARAH**'s arrival at school. She is displaced, lots of faces, lots of bodies, all of them busy, none of them noticing her.)*

*(The movement gets faster and faster until **ELEANOR** clocks her.)*

(Everything freezes.)

ELEANOR. Hello Sarah. I'm/

SARAH. Eleanor.

ELEANOR. Lady Butler of Kilkenny castle.

Have you been waiting long?

*(**SARAH** shakes her head.)*

Speak up.

SARAH. NO I WAS JUST WANDERING THE GARDEN ACTUALLY!

(Beat.)

ELEANOR. I'm sorry I couldn't come sooner.

I'm here now.

Shall we?

*(**SARAH** just stares at **ELEANOR**.)*

*(**ELEANOR** takes a step towards **SARAH**.)*

*(**SARAH** steps away.)*

Are you alright?

(**SARAH** *nods.*)

Sarah, I am to teach you languages.

Your words are important.

SARAH. I'm fine, thank you.

ELEANOR. Very good.

The library is this way.

Will you come with me?

(**SARAH** *nods.*)

(**ELEANOR** *looks at her disapprovingly.*)

SARAH. Yes, I will.

(*They walk into the library together.*)

(*Music plays* as people swarm around them again.*)

(*When they enter the library they are alone.*)

ELEANOR. What's that you're reading?

SARAH. Clarissa.

ELEANOR. Excellent choice.

SARAH. I could only find it in French.

ELEANOR. Parlez-vous français?

(**SARAH** *stares at her blankly.*)

SARAH. Oh. Sorry. Oui, merci.

Je suis très malade.

(**ELEANOR** *laughs.*)

ELEANOR.   Maintenant. On va commencer avec votre grammaire. Le pluriels, s'il vous plaît.

Je suis

(*Beat.*)

Tu es

Il est

Elle est

Nous sommes

(*Beat.*)

Tu ne peux pas parles le français?

SARAH. What?

(**ELEANOR** *laughs.*)

(*Beat.*)

There's another library you know.

Is there?

ELEANOR. They keep all the good stuff hidden. This one's mostly full of antiques. I think the English text is in there.

SARAH. Where is it?

ELEANOR. That would be telling, wouldn't it.

SARAH. Will you take me there?

ELEANOR. We aren't supposed to let students in.

SARAH. I won't tell anyone.

ELEANOR. And they'd all say the same.

SARAH. I want to read it.

ELEANOR. You'll have to wait.

SARAH. I have waited long enough!

> (**ELEANOR** *stares at her surprised.*)

Sorry.

Please will you show me.

> (**SARAH** *reads from her book in broken French.*)

Je ne connais pas mon coeur s'il n'est pas complètement libre.

I don't know what any of it means.

I just want to understand.

> (**ELEANOR** *exits.*)

> (**SARAH** *laughs.*)

SARAH. Now?!

> (**ELEANOR** *re-enters.*)

> (*She is carrying a book.*)

> (*Time has passed.*)

> (**SARAH** *runs towards her.*)

ELEANOR. Arrête!

D'abord en français

Changer le présent au passé composé, s'il vous plaît

Je suis

SARAH. Do we have to do this every time?!

ELEANOR. Je suis

SARAH. Really?

ELEANOR. Je suis!

>   *(Beat.)*

SARAH. J'ai été

ELEANOR. Tu est

SARAH. Tu as été

>   (**SARAH** *tries to grab the book again,*
>   **ELEANOR** *dismisses her.*)

ELEANOR. Nous sommes.

SARAH. Nous avons été

>   *(Again she tries and fails.)*

ELEANOR. Vous êtes

Ils sont

Elles sont.

>   *(This becomes somewhat of a game.)*
>
>   *(Both are increasingly amused.)*
>
>   (**ELEANOR** *begins to laugh and play with*
>   **SARAH.**)

SARAH. Vous avez été

Ils ont été

Elles ont été

>   *(Eventually* **SARAH** *catches* **ELEANOR,** *she
>   manages to pin her down and take the book
>   from her.)*
>
>   *(As soon as she has it she retreats into a
>   corner with it and starts reading, hungrily.)*

(**ELEANOR,** *startled by her sudden undoing, gets herself together and watches* **SARAH** *reading for a while.*)

What are you doing here?

ELEANOR. Read your book.

SARAH. Can't we speak?

ELEANOR. I'm not here for that.

SARAH. What are you here for then?

ELEANOR. To help you understand.

SARAH. What?

ELEANOR. The story.

SARAH. Which one?

ELEANOR. The one in that book.

SARAH. What about yours?

ELEANOR. Read.

(**SARAH** *laughs.*)

(**ELEANOR** *tries to ignore her and* **SARAH** *laughs louder.*)

What is so funny?

SARAH. I like this part.

ELEANOR. Which?

SARAH. Miss Howe to Clarissa.

ELEANOR. "How charmingly you and I may live together and despise them all"

SARAH. That's it.

(Beat.)

Carry on.

ELEANOR. I don't remember any more.

> *(Pause.)*

SARAH. I know who you are, you know.

ELEANOR. Oh, do you now?

SARAH. You're from one of the richest families in Ireland.

You're hiding out here pretending to be a teacher's aide.

ELEANOR. I always rather fancied a career in education.

SARAH. Bollocks.

ELEANOR. Sarah Ponsonby I will not hear another word that doesn't come directly from that book!!

> *(Beat.)*

SARAH. Do you like this story?

Do you?

ELEANOR. It's my favourite actually.

SARAH. The words are faded.

I can't understand them.

Read it to me.

That's why you're here, isn't it?

To help me understand.

> *(**SARAH** continues trying to read.)*

> *(**ELEANOR** watches her.)*

ELEANOR. If she be a woman, and love me, I shall surely catch her once tripping: for love was ever a traitor to its harbourer: and love within, and I without, she will be more than a woman, as the poet says, or I less than man, if I succeed not.

SARAH. And by my soul, I can neither eat, drink, nor sleep; nor, what's still worse, love any woman in the world but her.

(*Beat.*)

ELEANOR. Je ne connais pas mon coeur s'il n'est pas complètement libre.

SARAH. I know not my own heart if it be not absolutely free.

(*Beat.*)

ELEANOR. They sent me away.

SARAH. Why?

(*Beat.*)

ELEANOR. I did not belong where I was.

SARAH. So they sent you here?

ELEANOR. It was either here or a nunnery, and fuck that.

(**SARAH** *bursts out laughing, shocked at her sudden outburst.*)

SARAH. You're like me, aren't you?

(*Pause.*)

(*A moment of silence between them.*)

(**POSTMAN** *enters.*)

POSTMAN. Lady Butler.

(**ELEANOR**, *startled by the interruption, pulls herself from the moment quickly – back into teacher mode.*)

(There is something strange and uncomfortable in the air, but none of them know what it is.)

I apologise for the interruption.

ELEANOR. That's quite alright, we were finishing.

POSTMAN. I've a letter for Miss Ponsonby.

(He stands in the doorway, unsure what to do.)

ELEANOR. You'd best give it to her then.

POSTMAN. Oh right, yes, very good so.

*(He gives it to **SARAH**.)*

From Sir William Fownes at Woodstock, Miss.

SARAH. Thank you.

*(**POSTMAN** exits.)*

*(**SARAH** opens letter and reads.)*

ELEANOR. Everything alright?

SARAH. My Aunt is unwell.

ELEANOR. What will you do?

SARAH. I have to go back, don't I?

ELEANOR. Do you?

SARAH. Can I write to you?

(Beat.)

ELEANOR. Yes.

*(**ELEANOR** writes down a note on a piece of paper.)*

Use this address.

SARAH. The post office?

ELEANOR. Postage there is received only by myself.

SARAH. But that's miles away.

ELEANOR. I know.

SARAH. But –

ELEANOR. We must be careful about all this.

Very careful.

Do you understand?

>   (**SARAH** *nods, unsure.*)

You will write though?

SARAH. Every day.

And you will write back?

ELEANOR. Yes.

>   (*Beat.*)

Now.

>   (**ELEANOR** *goes to leave.*)
>
>   (**SARAH** *stares after her.*)
>
>   (**ELEANOR** *shouts.*)

This is the part where you follow me!

>   (**SARAH** *runs to follow her.*)

Scene Six

Woodstock, Kilkenny

(SIR WILLIAM enters.)

SIR WILLIAM. Sarah!

(SARAH runs in, breathless.)

You are returned to us.

SARAH. I came as quickly as I could.

SIR WILLIAM. So I see.

SARAH. May I see her?

SIR WILLIAM. She is resting.

Come here to me.

SARAH. I have had rather a long journey.

(He gestures to her.)

SIR WILLIAM. How are you finding school?

SARAH. Most enjoyable, thank you.

SIR WILLIAM. I hear you are making great strides with your languages.

SARAH. I am well taught.

SIR WILLIAM. So I hear.

Many an hour spent over in the staff library with Lady Eleanor of Kilkenny.

SARAH. How did you –

SIR WILLIAM. People write, you know.

SARAH. Oh.

(Beat.)

SIR WILLIAM. Lady Betty will be pleased to see you anyway.

SARAH. And I her.

SIR WILLIAM. She has not done well without you, if truth be told.

Nor have any of us, for that matter.

You have been much missed.

SARAH. Have I?

SIR WILLIAM. Now, if you'll accompany me – supper will be just served I think.

SARAH. I shall return to my room, I am rather tired.

(Beat.)

SIR WILLIAM. Sarah, are you unwell?

SARAH. No, I'm fine.

SIR WILLIAM. Something is... changed here.

SARAH. It is not.

SIR WILLIAM. Don't answer back.

*(***SARAH*** stops talking.)*

We shall expect you early for breakfast tomorrow then.

If it's not too much trouble, of course.

SARAH. Of course not.

(He stands over her.)

SIR WILLIAM. How very precious you are to us all.

(He exits.)

*(***SARAH*** laughs and the following words burst out of her.)*

SARAH. He knows!

He knows, he knows he must know.

> *(She puts her hands to her mouth.)*

My love !

> *(She tries to catch the words but they keep spilling out.)*

My love!

My love!

My love!

> *(She grabs a pen and paper.)*

Dear Eleanor

Rose today at six. Walked the rose garden, the Lilys were in full bloom. How lovely they were in the early light. Lady Betty resting, I will visit with her tomorrow. Read Lettres de Deux Amans, Rousseau. Managed some of the translation, not all.

Enclosed is a short passage that I hoped you may help me understand.

Each day I stand at the door, burning.

Each day there are no words from you is death to me.

> Sarah scribbles out the last two lines and instead she writes;

With sincerest affections,

S.P.

> *(**LADY BETTY** enters.)*

LADY BETTY. There you are!

SARAH. My Lady, you should be in bed!

LADY BETTY. I am well aware.

Did you not hear me call?

SARAH. No?

LADY BETTY. Gone a bit deaf these days it seems.

SARAH. I'm sorry. I was writing.

LADY BETTY. Very dedicated study, aren't you?

> (**LADY BETTY** *walks towards her, stumbles.*)

Come now dear, help an old lady.

SARAH. Come here to me.

> (**LADY BETTY** *sits down awkwardly.*)

LADY BETTY. I'm too old for all this.

I got closer, you know, this time.

Too close, really.

You'd have noticed it, if you'd been here.

I looked well.

Big round belly.

Always such a mess after.

He won't come near me now.

Says I'm cursed.

> (**SARAH** *does not know what to say.*)

Oh, a letter came for you yesterday, Master Edward the post gave it to me by mistake.

> (**ELEANOR** *appears.*)

ELEANOR. My Dear Sarah.

LADY BETTY. He really does offer a rather mediocre service, doesn't he?

ELEANOR. Forgive the delay in response – I have not had a moment's rest for composing my reply, much as I did want to.

LADY BETTY. Now, tell me what's been going on while you've been away. I have been kept in suspense.

ELEANOR. It has warmed my heart to hear of your garden, I do so miss the colours of my own grounds at this time of year. Is there much lavender at Woodstock? That is my favourite.

LADY BETTY. Sir William said you are much improved with your French.

ELEANOR. Perhaps you could bring a small bundle back for us here?

LADY BETTY. Sarah?

SARAH. I have been reading a lot in the evenings.

LADY BETTY. Oh yes?

ELEANOR. I was most pleased to hear you have started reading Lettres de Deux Amans, or, for the correct translation/ *(The next few lines are said in unison with* **SARAH.***)* Letters of two lovers.

SARAH. Letters of two lovers.

LADY BETTY. Any good?

ELEANOR & SARAH. It is one of my favourites.

ELEANOR. To clarify the narrative for your understanding, the passage you have included is spoken in secret correspondence between Julie, our young ingenue, and the villain of our story, Saint Preux, who Julie's Mother has recently employed to become her tutor.

The translation, as per your request, is as follows.

"I tremble as often as our hands meet, and I know not how it happens, but they meet constantly. I start as soon as I feel the touch of your finger; I am seized with a fever, or rather delirium, in these sports; my senses gradually forsake me; and when I am thus beside myself what can I say, what can I do, where hide myself, how be answerable for my behaviour?"

Soon after these words are spoken, Julie and Saint Preux are united as one flesh.

Julie's Mother of course, upon learning this, dies of grief.

> (**SARAH** *jumps up and gasps.*)

> (**ELEANOR** *exits.*)

LADY BETTY. SARAH!

> (**SARAH** *suddenly embraces* **LADY BETTY**, *hysterical.*)

SARAH. There is something very wrong with me!

LADY BETTY. Sarah. Stop it. Stop it now!

> (**LADY BETTY** *removes* **SARAH** *from her.*)

Where on earth has this come from?

Has something happened?

> (**SARAH** *says nothing.*)

Are you unhappy at school?

> (**SARAH** *shakes her head.*)

Has someone here upset you?

> (*And again, furiously.*)

You have been driven quite to distraction all week. I haven't known at all what to do with you. Truth be told it's been most upsetting.

SARAH. I am sorry.

I am so sorry.

LADY BETTY. Yes, that's enough of that now, thank you.

I am going back to bed then.

I am rather fragile and I was nearly hopeful for a moment's peace here.

SARAH. May I join you for breakfast?

LADY BETTY. If you could do so without hysterics, that would be much appreciated.

And then I think it may be time for you to return to your studies.

No use having you hanging around here pitying me.

Quite enough of that from my husband.

(**LADY BETTY** *exits.*)

(**SARAH** *runs back to her writing.*)

SARAH. Dear Eleanor.

What joy to receive your letter, please do not worry about it's delay. I barely noticed. I have actually been very busy myself in restoring my poor Lady Betty to health. What a joy it has been to care for her in her hour of need, as she has done many times for me in childhood.

I am writing this letter with good news in hand – my Lady Betty is much improved and bid me return to school immediately.

How happy it shall make me to be with you again!!

(*She crosses it out.*)

To be back in school again.

I must finish writing now and start my packing.

P.s Thank you for the translation of text – one question, when you mentioned Julie and her handsome tutor are "united as one flesh" – what exactly did you mean?

As I am not well acquainted with this term, I think perhaps a more detailed description would be helpful.

Sent with most dearest affections

S.P.

(As music plays, the tender connection between **SARAH** *and* **ELEANOR** *grows through their correspondence. Letters written, sent, received, desire growing, tenderness building – a deep dark secret.)*

Scene Seven

Woodstock, Kilkenny

(SIR WILLIAM *enters and stops* SARAH *in her tracks.*)

SIR WILLIAM. You are leaving us, then?

SARAH. Lady Betty said –

SIR WILLIAM. I know what Lady Betty said.

(*Beat.*)

She's not well, you know.

SARAH. She seems better.

SIR WILLIAM. Women can turn without much notice.

SARAH. I can stay –

SIR WILLIAM. No, no.

You toddle off now, back to your friend.

(*Beat.*)

Sarah, come here to me.

SARAH. I must pack –

SIR WILLIAM. It will wait.

(*Beat.*)

(SARAH *turns to him.*)

Sarah, have I done something to cause all this?

SARAH. Sorry?

SIR WILLIAM. This... silence of late. Scuttling about the place under cover of darkness and such.

You must know people are talking.

SARAH. Oh.

SIR WILLIAM. I'd half wondered whether it was perhaps something to do with... me?

SARAH. Oh, no my Lord.

SIR WILLIAM. Every time I enter a room you jump ten feet in the air.

I thought we had passed all that.

SARAH. I'm sorry.

(Beat.)

SIR WILLIAM. You can talk to me, you know.

About anything.

Nothing is off limits here.

SARAH. Thank you.

SIR WILLIAM. I am most fond of you Sarah.

SARAH. And I you.

SIR WILLIAM. Really?

SARAH. Of course.

SIR WILLIAM. Well, that's the most wonderful news.

(Beat.)

Now, this new tie.

What do you think, does it suit me?

It's a new style, from France. I am told the young gentlemen of Paris are sporting it such.

Is it becoming of me?

You don't seem convinced.

SARAH. I'm sure it would be it's just a bit –

SIR WILLIAM. Yes?

SARAH. Well it's a bit... crooked?!

SIR WILLIAM. Damn it all to Hades. You're right. I've been following a drawing sent but I've yet to master the knotage.

> *(He fumbles with it.)*

Blast these stubby little hoof hands.

Would you mind awfully...

> *(**SARAH** goes to help him.)*

> *(A moment of silence while she fixes his tie.)*

Important to keep abreast of the fashions, I think.

> *(**SARAH** plays with his tie throughout the following section.)*

I am a man of not fifty years.

Virile still, rather sprightly I am told.

A fine hand in the gene pool I have been dealt.

Yet still no son and heir.

And no wife who can give it to me.

Not yet.

> *(**SIR WILLIAM** leans in, grabs **SARAH**'s behind and kisses her without her consent. Tries to put his tongue in her mouth. **SARAH** freezes. Then she struggles to get away.)*

> *(Eventually she manages to push him off her and falls to the floor in shock.)*

(If there are witnesses present on stage, they turn away.)

I'm sorry my love, did I shock you?

(SARAH looks up at him, horrified.)

You wanted that.

(Beat.)

You've always wanted that.

(Beat.)

Look at you there.

On your knees.

Like a hungry dog.

SARAH. You're disgusting.

SIR WILLIAM. And you're an ungrateful little bitch.

Someone else's child.

Someone else's waste.

What the hell did you think I was keeping you here for?

ANSWER ME YOU STUPID LITTLE GIRL!

If I'd have known I'd be met with this attitude, I'd have left you to the orphanage where you belonged.

(Beat.)

Get up.

Get up.

(SARAH gets up.)

You shall be returned to your schooling.

I will decide what happens to you next.

(He leaves.)

(**SARAH** *gets up, tries to speak.)*

(She cannot.)

(She runs away.)

Scene Eight

Miss Parkes School for Girls

(Music* as **SARAH** *runs back to the people, back to school.)*

(She stands in the middle of the space.)

(All stare at her.)

(She motions like she is going to be violently sick, then she screams very loudly.)

(The witnesses leave in fear.)

*(***ELEANOR** *does not leave.)*

ELEANOR. Sarah.

*(***SARAH** *cannot speak.)*

*(***ELEANOR** *takes a step towards* **SARAH,** **SARAH** *backs away from her.)*

What has happened to you?

Can you tell me?

Can you –

*(***ELEANOR** *tries again to step to* **SARAH,** **SARAH** *flinches.)*

OK.

You just stay there then.

---

* A licence to produce CELEBRATED VIRGINS does not include a performance licence for any third-party or copyrighted music. Licensees should create an original composition or use music in the public domain. For further information, please see Music Use Note on page iii.

I'll stay here.

I'll stay just here.

I'll not go.

>*(Silence.)*

>*(Then.)*

SARAH. If I speak, will you hear me?

ELEANOR. Yes, of course.

SARAH. But will you listen?

If I speak in my own words.

>**(ELEANOR** *nods.)*

SARAH. I will decide what happens next.

>*(Beat.)*

SARAH. Eleanor, I love you.

>*(Beat.)*

Did you hear me?

>**(ELEANOR** *nods.)*

But do you understand?

>**(ELEANOR** *nods again.)*

Your words are important

>*(Beat.)*

>**(ELEANOR** *writes something down and hands it to* **SARAH.***)*

ELEANOR. We can't stay here.

SARAH. Why not?

ELEANOR. It's not safe.

SARAH. Where is safe?

ELEANOR. I don't know.

>*(**SARAH** tries to leave.)*

We can't just run.

SARAH. We literally can, there's the door.

ELEANOR. Sarah, do you know who I am?

>Do you know what this is?

>Do you understand what will happen if we/

SARAH. Entirely. And I want it. All of it. Now.

>*(Beat.)*

ELEANOR. Go back.

SARAH. But I want to stay with you.

ELEANOR. I know.

>But if we do this right we can leave.

>Together.

>I will send word, and I will come to you.

SARAH. How?

ELEANOR. I don't know that yet.

SARAH. Where are we going?

ELEANOR. I don't know.

SARAH. What will we do there?

ELEANOR. I have no idea.

But we will be there together.

Could that be enough?

(**SARAH** *takes* **ELEANOR***'s hand.*)

SARAH.　Now?!

(*They run.*)

(**SARAH** *returned to Woodstock.*)

(**SIR WILLIAM** *welcomes her. We see her hide from him, we see a map arrive, we see the pistol, the hats, the window.*)

(**SARAH** *jumps.*)

(**ELEANOR** *is waiting for her.*)

(*They leave.*)

(*They make as far as the port, but there is a storm.*)

(*The boat doesn't sail.*)

Scene Nine

Woodstock, Kilkenny

(SIR WILLIAM enters, tears open a letter.)

SIR WILLIAM. BETTY.

(LADY BETTY enters.)

LADY BETTY. Have they found her?

SIR WILLIAM. No.

LADY BETTY. Have they searched the gardens?

SIR WILLIAM. The entire grounds apparently.

No trace.

LADY BETTY. I don't understand.

SIR WILLIAM. No, Lady Betty, it appears you do not.

LADY BETTY. Where else could she be?

SIR WILLIAM. I was rather hoping you were going to help me out with that one.

Or do we have to draw this pathetic little act out further?

LADY BETTY. What do you mean?

SIR WILLIAM. Do you take me for a fool?

The pair of you have been planning this for months, haven't you?

She wanted rid of me and you wanted rid of her.

It's true isn't it?

LADY BETTY. No.

SIR WILLIAM. Isn't it?

LADY BETTY. No!

> (**SIR WILLIAM** *stands near her, threatening violence.*)

SIR WILLIAM. Tell me the truth you wretched old woman!

LADY BETTY. I honestly don't know where she is!

SIR WILLIAM. Really?

Well then this situation is even more dire than you thought.

Read this.

> (*He throws a letter at her feet.*)

Miss Parkes writes here that she was forced to send another letter this morning, to Kilkenny castle.

LADY BETTY. Why?

SIR WILLIAM. Lady Eleanor Butler, first daughter of Kilkenny is similarly absconded.

No one in the school has seen trace of her for days.

Miss Parkes has reason to believe they are together.

Her parents have sent out their own search party, who are now combing the port docks.

And they themselves are on their way here.

LADY BETTY. What will we tell them?

SIR WILLIAM. You'd better be able to tell them that she is found, hadn't you?

LADY BETTY. But I don't know where she is.

SIR WILLIAM. Then you'd better start bloody well thinking fast.

Or God knows what'll become of us all next.

Go on, off you go.

Not going to track her down standing there, are you?

(He goes to leave and then he turns.)

It's probably a good job you were never a mother, isn't it?

*(**SIR WILLIAM** and **LADY BETTY** exit.)*

Scene Ten

A Barn Outside Waterford Port

(SARAH *and* ELEANOR *are alone in a barn.* SARAH *is unwell.* ELEANOR *is pacing up and down,* SARAH *watches her.*)

ELEANOR. I can't believe I've brought you here.

SARAH. I know, it's a most violent kidnapping, I'm terrified of you.

ELEANOR. Stop it.

SARAH. They can't just keep the boat there in the harbour, it'll have to set sail tomorrow.

ELEANOR. You've been saying that for days.

Sarah, look at you, you're shaking.

SARAH. I'm fine.

(ELEANOR *goes to* SARAH *and holds her.*)

ELEANOR. We need to get you to a doctor.

SARAH. And where are we going to find one of those, in the pig sty?

(SARAH *takes* ELEANOR*'s face.*)

(*Beat.*)

(ELEANOR *breaks down.*)

ELEANOR. I don't know what I thought was going to happen here. Twenty three miles to the nearest port.

I've never ridden a horse in my life.

Never even been on a boat.

I just thought –

If they find us –

SARAH. I know.

ELEANOR. There is a good chance that they will.

SARAH. Let them.

ELEANOR. Sarah, you don't understand.

SARAH. I do, I just don't care.

ELEANOR. Aren't you scared?

SARAH. No.

No, actually I'm really not.

Not anymore.

This part.

I like this.

Je ne connais pas mon coeur s'il n'est pas complètement libre.

(**SARAH** *goes to kiss* **ELEANOR**.)

(*A loud knock is heard on the barn door.*)

Scene Eleven

A Carriage Outside Waterford Port

(**LADY BETTY, ELEANOR** *and* **SARAH** *sit in the carriage in silence.*)

(**SARAH** *is collapsed into* **LADY BETTY.**)

(**LADY BETTY** *holds her.*)

LADY BETTY. Are you going to explain yourself or shall we sit here in silence forever?

(*Beat.*)

HELLO?

ELEANOR. I'm very sorry.

LADY BETTY. Are you?

ELEANOR. Yes.

LADY BETTY. Do you have any idea what you've done?

And I'm sorry, forgive me for the intrusion but might I ask what on earth you were planning on doing with my child if I'd not come to find her?

(*Beat.*)

Well?

ELEANOR. We were to retire from society.

LADY BETTY. Where?

ELEANOR. We were to tour across the North.

Find a house.

LADY BETTY. By what means?

ELEANOR. I have money.

LADY BETTY. Oh, do you now?

ELEANOR. Yes. I'm from a very good family.

LADY BETTY. Do you know, I honestly can't decide if you're entirely stupid or just spoilt.

Doesn't really matter to you though, does it?

Your surname and the standing you were born into clears you from any real consequence.

She isn't like you though, is she?

She is an orphan, are you even aware of that?

All Sarah has is her reputation and hopes of a successful marriage.

> *(Beat.)*

ELEANOR. What happens now?

LADY BETTY. I am going to take my child home, where she is safe.

ELEANOR. What about me?

LADY BETTY. Drive on please.

> *(The* **COACH** *starts moving.)*

> *(They move in silence for a while. Then voice and sound from off.)*

COACH MAN. Hold that coach! Hold I say! Hold!

LADY BETTY. Stop the car!

> *(***MAN** *approaches.)*

Not one word from either one of you.

> *(***COACHMAN** *enters the carriage.)*

COACH MAN. Good morning Lady Betty.

(**LADY BETTY** *nods at the man.*)

Lady Eleanor, I am sent by your Father to return you to Kilkenny immediately. The coach is waiting. Into the car with you please.

(**ELEANOR** *does not move.*)

Into the car, now.

(**ELEANOR** *does not move.*)

ELEANOR. No.

COACH MAN. I'm sorry?

ELEANOR. I'll not go.

COACH MAN. Very well then.

(**COACHMAN** *goes to leave.*)

LADY BETTY. For goodness sake Eleanor, enough.

There are armed men outside.

They will tear this carriage apart with Sarah inside it.

Have you still not caused her enough damage?

(**ELEANOR** *looks at* **SARAH.** *Then she stands up and goes with the* **COACHMAN.**)

LADY BETTY. Drive on please.

(*The* **COACH** *drives on. Music plays*.*)

---

* A licence to produce CELEBRATED VIRGINS does not include a performance licence for any third-party or copyrighted music. Licensees should create an original composition or use music in the public domain. For further information, please see Music Use Note on page iii.

Scene Twelve

Woodstock, Kilkenny

> (**LADY BETTY** *enters with* **SARAH** *collapsed on her.*)

SIR WILLIAM. You're back.

LADY BETTY. We are.

> (**LADY BETTY** *carries* **SARAH** *up the stairs,* **SIR WILLIAM** *goes to help her.*)

No!

You will not go any further.

SIR WILLIAM. I beg your pardon.

LADY BETTY. You will not touch her.

You will stay exactly where you are.

Do not take another step towards either of us.

SIR WILLIAM. Who do you think you are talking to?

LADY BETTY. Good question.

> (*Beat.*)

SIR WILLIAM. She's got into your head, hasn't she?

She doesn't know what she's talking about.

LADY BETTY. She knows far too well what she is talking about.

She has spoken it all to me.

And I heard her.

I'm sure others will too, if you'd like her to speak on it here.

> (**SIR WILLIAM** *cannot speak.*)

Yes, I thought as much.

Now go on, get out.

We will have no more from you.

There is no place for you here.

> (**SIR WILLIAM** *leaves.*)

Now.

> (**LADY BETTY** *enters with* **SARAH**, *puts her to bed. Leaves her. Passage of time,* **SARAH** *unmoving.*)

> (**LADY BETTY** *knocks on* **SARAH**'s *door.*)

Sarah. Sarah my love, may I come in?

> (*Beat.*)

I'm coming in.

> (**LADY BETTY** *enters the room.*)

I brought you some hot tea.

Cools you down apparently.

> (*Offers* **SARAH** *a cup of tea. She does not take it.* **LADY BETTY** *takes a sip. Chokes.*)

Bit hot that, actually. I'll just pop it over here for a while shall I? Let it cool for you.

> (*She sets down the tea.*)

Let's have a look at you.

> (**LADY BETTY** *puts her hand on* **SARAH**'s *head. As soon as she touches her* **SARAH** *dissolves into desolate tears.*)

Oh Sarah. Oh now. Come on, my love. Please.

Enough of this.

She will be well enough.

She is from the richest family in Ireland.

> (**SARAH** *tries to get up, fails, she is delirious and fragile.*)

Sarah, please! Stop it! Lie down.

> (**LADY BETTY** *grapples with* **SARAH** *and lies her back down.* **SARAH** *crumples back onto the bed.*)

You must stop this mania. You are not well enough for it. You are going to drive yourself to an early grave.

> (*Pause.*)

Sarah, I am honestly at a loss as to what to do here.

Are you lonely, is that it?

Do you have any other friends?

I could perhaps write to Mrs Goddard and ask her if Siobhan could come over and sit with you a while. She likes reading too, I am told.

> (*Beat.*)

I'm afraid I don't understand any of this.

But I do love you, you know. Very much.

Thought we'd never see you again.

Thought the sky would cave in.

But, there we are.

You're here now.

Things pass dear.

Everything passes.

>   *(Beat.)*

Now let's have a feel of that tea.

>   (**BETTY** *picks up the tea and sips it.*)

Ah yes, that's lovely now.

Will you?

>   (**LADY BETTY** *offers* **SARAH** *some tea. She turns
>   away.*)

I'll leave you to rest then.

I shall be in my room should you need me. I shall be up
a while battling with my cross stitch, I'd wager. You've
only to ring that if you need me.

>   (**LADY BETTY** *leaves a bell. Goes to leave.*)

SARAH. I love you too.

BETTY. Drink that tea then.

>   (**BETTY** *leaves.*)

>   (**SARAH** *sits up in bed, eventually drinks a
>   small sip of tea.*)

>   (*As she does so, we see a hand appear in the
>   window.* **SARAH** *jumps out of her skin, spills
>   her tea.*)

>   (**ELEANOR**'s *face appear at the window. She
>   gestures desperately for* **SARAH** *to open the
>   window.*)

>   (**SARAH** *gets up and attempts to open the
>   window.*)

(ELEANOR clambers through. She is exhausted, dishevelled and out of breath.)

ELEANOR. *(Mouthing.)* That's... Very... High... ⌐

SARAH. Shhhhh!

(They stare at each other.)

(Whispering.) What are you doing here?

ELEANOR. They were going to send me to a convent!

SARAH. Fuck that!

ELEANOR. I know!

(They hold each other.)

SARAH. How did you –?

*(A **SERVANT** is heard.)*

SERVANT. Miss Sarah?

Miss Sarah, are you alright?

*(**SARAH** and **ELEANOR** look at each other.)*

SARAH. Climb back outside.

ELEANOR. That's no good, they'll be watching.

SERVANT. I'm coming in.

SARAH. Hold on a second I/

ELEANOR. Sarah, let him come.

Enough of this.

*(**SERVANT** enters and stands in shock.)*

SARAH. We don't have to tell anyone. She will be gone. Tomorrow. You can just pretend this never happened, we can all keep quiet and -

SERVANT. Keep quiet ? Are you - I can't - I can't lose this job. I've got a family Miss. I've got children.

ELEANOR. I am from the richest family in Ireland. You wouldn't want to piss me off either.

(LADY BETTY *enters.*)

LADY BETTY. What on earth is going on?

(*Silence.*)

Ah. I see you've met our guest. Lady Eleanor of Kilkenny will be staying with us tonight, I'm sorry the house were not informed, it was all rather last minute.

SERVANT. That's quite alright Miss –

LADY BETTY. Did you need something?

SERVANT. I came to see if everything was alright.

I heard voices, I didn't know/

LADY BETTY. Well, now you do know.

SERVANT. Yes my Lady.

LADY BETTY. Family well?

SERVANT. Oh yes, they're fine thank you.

LADY BETTY. Happy here?

SERVANT. Very much so, thank you.

LADY BETTY. Best to keep all of this quiet then.

Goodnight.

SERVANT. Goodnight Lady Betty.

(SERVANT *leaves.*)

LADY BETTY. I shall see you for breakfast in the morning.

Lady Eleanor will not be here.

(LADY BETTY leaves.)

(The community cast enter to see what is going on.)

SARAH. Are you listening now?

(To ELEANOR.)

Take my hand, my love.

(SARAH takes ELEANOR's hand.)

(They stand centre stage.)

(All the witnesses hear her.)

My name is Miss Sarah Ponsonby!

It is my sole intention to live and die with Lady Eleanor Butler!

And nothing shall detract me from my purpose.

(SARAH turns to ELEANOR.)

What do we do now?

(She suddenly notices everyone is looking at them.)

ELEANOR. We run.

(LADY BETTY enters.)

LADY BETTY. Sarah?

Sarah?

Sarah, where are you my love?

(SARAH looks back at LADY BETTY.)

SARAH. Can I just –

ELEANOR. No.

Now.

Or not at all.

SARAH. Now.

(They run.)

(Blackout.)

End of Act One

ACT TWO

Scene One

Plas Newydd, Llangollen

(During the interval, the witnesses make and tend to the garden, turning the stage into Plas Newydd, Llangollen.)

(There should be flowers, colour, nature everywhere.)

*(When the stage is ready and the audience is still getting settled, **MARY CARYLL** enters – like a bull in a china shop. Encumbered with a number of domestic tasks – carrying suitcases, covered in flour, dead turkey in her hand, sweating.)*

(Makes her way to the stage, on her way she takes a sip from an audience member's drink, decides she likes it and takes the whole thing up onto stage with her. She gets up to the stage, downs the drink and demands silence.)

MARY CARYLL. OI!

OI! SHUT UP I'M TALKING NOW!

It's my bit.

Now.

Two things to say before we kick this bit off, firstly I am sorry I'm a bit late to the proceedings this evening. Only I've been a bit BUSY.

Which leads me swimmingly on to the second thing –

Enjoyed the first bit did you, yeah?

Rooting for them both weren't you, having a little cry, yeah?

Yeah I saw you.

Right, got a little question for you though before we go on any further that I am sure you won't have considered...

WHO'S CARRYING ALL THE BAGS THEN?

Well?

Well?

(She asks an audience member specifically.)

Yeah that's right! /Nope, try again *(Depending on answer.)* Packhorse Mary over here.

That's the thing about these stories innit... Roaring and riding and kissing and crying but no one has to hoof a bloody thing. Have you noticed? Not one messy undercarriage. Everyone's had their dinner.

Do you know why?

Me, that's why.

Mucking out the chamber pots!

Banging out the skidmarks!

Bleeding out this turkey and plucking it quick before it gets rigor mortis!

Messy little jobs.

Scene always changes before it gets to them bits though, doesn't it?

Didn't pay to watch old Mary doing her clean up act, did we? Someone's got to though, ain't they?

Oh don't you mind me dear, you have your existential crisis, I'll just be over here peeling the carrots so nobody gets scurvy while you're at it.

(Mocking their accents.)

Oh...oh...are we in love are we?

Searching for yourself are you?

Yeah?

Well, do you know what I am?

Well?

No! Guess again!

I'm FLATARSE KNACKERED.

What am I?

> *(She asks the man in question again. Hopefully he will respond with "Flatarse knackered".)*

Yeah. That's it. See, he's learning.

> *(She sits.)*

I wouldn't have minded a lover you know.

I think I'd have been good at it.

Sturdy woman I am.

Buxom.

Well balanced.

Good with me hands.

Wouldn't have minded a bit of carnal knowledge while I'm roasting the old spit.

Not much doing round here though.

Only Master Barry in the garden.

More meat on a rind of bacon.

I'd snap him in half, the poor fucker.

> *(Beat.)*

Now, don't get me wrong – I've got a lot of love for those two ladies in there.

I do.

Go to the ends of the earth for them I would.

And I did.

Knock on my door, two in the bloody morning;

"Mary, do you fancy a change of scenery?"

Off we went, Dawn's crack, straight over the Irish Sea, stomach like a sewer pit –

Off the boat, suitcases out, huffing and puffing behind them two taking in the vistas, staring into each other's eyes – and there's me bumbling about the place for three weeks until

"Ooo... Eleanor. What do you think?"

 'Yes dear. This'll do nicely."

Larn... Llan...

Wales.

Good enough place as any.

And I'd do it all again.

I'm not complaining.

Happy as a pig in the proverbial me.

I mean, would you look at this place?!

It's just, well...

Look me up in the history books and you know what it says?

"Mary Caryll. Loyal domestic servant all her life. Portly of stature and red of face. History unknown."

Yeah, well... I didn't have time to write any of it down, did I ?

So, you just clock that,

Right?

All of this –

I was there too.

And I'm still here.

Mary Caryll.

Remember that.

Come and see me anytime you like.

(Turns to the man again.)

I'm on the spit at six.

(She leaves.)

Scene Two

Plas Newydd Garden

(The stage opens up to reveal a beautiful, colourful garden.)

(There are flowers everywhere.)

(SARAH sits amongst them.)

(ELEANOR enters.)

ELEANOR. What's that one called ?

SARAH. Alstroemeria.

The flower of achieved aspirations.

ELEANOR. Bold claim!

(SARAH laughs.)

SARAH. How's Daisy?

ELEANOR Stubborn as ever. Farmer Morgan tried to milk her early this morning, came out covered in more filth than the pigs.

SARAH. That's our girl.

(ELEANOR sits with SARAH.)

(SARAH plays with her hair.)

(They breath in the fresh air together.)

ELEANOR Joyous day.

What's happening in school right now, do you think?

SARAH. Sun's about to go down, mass will be starting.

ELEANOR Ah yes.

A good two hour shower.

Father Finnegan spraying out Latin prayers over the pews.

I miss him terribly, don't you?

SARAH. Every time it rains.

(*They laugh together.*)

Oh, look, there's that butcher's wife again.

(**SARAH** *stands to look at her.*)

She passes by here most afternoons, I think she might live across the field.

I don't know her name, do you?

ELEANOR. No.

SARAH. We should make ourselves known to her, she'll be good for the pigs.

Hello! Helloooo!

(**SARAH** *waves.*)

ELEANOR. Sarah, stop that!

SARAH. Can't I even say hello to her?

ELEANOR. You can say whatever you want.

Just don't bring me into it.

SARAH. I think that ship has sailed, don't you?

People are asking to see us, you know.

ELEANOR. Did we invite them or are we opening up an exhibition?

I can see them, you know. They think they're being subtle, well they're bloody well not.

Sundays, market days, eyes poking up in bushes.

Staring like we've got three heads.

SARAH. We're the ones that moved here.

Onto their land.

Their town.

We are living in a house that their Fathers built.

ELEANOR. Vultures stalking for a pound of flesh.

SARAH. You do know what they are calling us, don't you?

ELEANOR. No?

SARAH. The Hermitesses of the Vale.

ELEANOR. Hemitesses?!

SARAH. Apparently so.

ELEANOR. Where was that?

SARAH. This month's chronicle.

ELEANOR. How dare they! They have no idea who we are!

SARAH. Perhaps a good time to show them then.

Evidence otherwise.

ELEANOR. Do I look like a science specimen?

SARAH. People are interested.

(**SARAH** *puts the flower in* **ELEANOR***'s hair.*)

Not everyone gets to live as we do, you know.

We are so lucky, my love.

Look at where we are.

What we have made.

Our garden.

Our life.

Isn't it beautiful?

ELEANOR. Yes, so we must keep it safe.

I came here to be with you.

In peace.

SARAH. And we shall be.

If we get this part right.

Nearly there now.

 (Beat.)

ELEANOR. Are there many requests for an audience?

 *(**SARAH** pulls handfuls of letters out of her pocket.)*

Christ.

SARAH. Mary. Mary dear!

 *(**ELEANOR** exits.)*

MARY. *(From offstage.)* Oh for JESUS SAKE!

Scene Three

Plas Newydd, Llangollen

(The ladies sit to their writing.)

SARAH. My dear friend, forgive the delay in correspondence, we have been most busy with renovations of the grounds. However, it gives me great joy to tell you all is blooming beautifully and it would be our greatest pleasure to accept your offer of a visit, should you have time to pass by our small bower.

ELEANOR. Expenses February – Clogmaker sent to Wrexham for nothing, three shillings. Hair powder three shillings. Mary discharged from kitchen for having the itch, seven shillings. Mr Ballis' shameless demand of nine pounds reduced to a still unreasonable six pound two shillings. Peggy for working over while Mary was under cure from the itch, three shillings.

(Voices are heard.)

CHARLES MATTHEWS. I have to-day at last received an invitation to call, if I have time as I pass, at Llangollen, to be received in due form, from the dear old gentlemen called Lady Butler and Miss Ponsonby.

MRS PIOZZI. Have at last received my long awaited invitation for an audience with the local hermitesses.

ANNA SEWARD. I resume my pen, to speak to you of that enchanting unique, in conduct and situation, of which we have all heard so much, though, as yet, without distinct description. You will guess that I mean the celebrated ladies of Llangollen Vale.

> *(The guests make their way to make their way to Plas Newydd.)*

(**SARAH** *and* **ELEANOR** *preparing for guests.*)

ELEANOR. You're sure about this then, are you?

SARAH. Not entirely.

Can't hurt to give it a try though, can it?

ELEANOR. Let's hope not.

How long before they get here, do you think?

SARAH. Lord knows.

ELEANOR. Enough time for la grammaire, do you think ?

SARAH. Absolutely not.

ELEANOR. Je Suis.

SARAH. Stop it.

ELEANOR. J'ai été

SARAH. Any more of that and I shall chase you down to la rivière.

(*Beat.*)

ELEANOR. Nous Sommes.

SARAH. Right then.

(**SARAH** *chases* **ELEANOR**, *playfully.*)

(**MARY** *enters and disturbs them.*)

(*She has with her several guests, who stare at the Ladies.*)

(*The guests should be represented by the same witnesses who up until now have not been allowed to enter the story.*)

MARY. Mr Charles Matthews of Plymouth.

ELEANOR. Come in, you are most welcome.

Miss Seward of Lichfield.

Mrs Piozzi of Caernarfonshire

> *(Arrival of guests at Plas Newydd. The ladies sitting do dinner, laughing, listening with amusement, boredom, anger, dining, bored, squeezing each other's hand under the table.)*

> *(More guests arrive.)*

MARY. Lord Hanmer of Flint.

Lady Stanley of Derby.

Bernard.

> *(The guests leave. They close the door.)*

ELEANOR. How did I do?

> *(**SARAH** walks up to **ELEANOR** and kisses her on the cheek.)*

SARAH. I think you're wonderful.

ELEANOR. I know that.

What about them?

> *(**MARY** enters with another woman.)*

MARY. Lady Dungannon, countess of Fermanagh.

LADY DUNGANNON. Good evening.

SARAH. Welcome good Lady, will you come in?

> *(They entertain Lady Dungannon.)*

> *(Voices are heard again from off again.)*

CHARLES. Well, it has happened at last. I have seen them, heard them, touched them. The pets, 'the ladies', as they are called, the curiosities of Llangollen.

ANNA SEWARD. By their own invitation, I drank tea with them thrice during the nine days of my visit to Wales; and, by their kind introduction, partook of a rural dinner, given by their maid Mary.

MRS PIOZZI. Wandering towards the Glen that day soon discovered a Gothic Cottage; I was tremblingly diffident and afraid till I found the door wide open, a female beckoned me, so that I entered with confidence and found myself in a most heavenly Retreat – a convent in miniature.

LADY STANLEY. Their abode is quite a little paradise, though I was rather disappointed in the situation; but the ladies did not disappoint me, though they did not answer many of my questions.

(**LADY DUNGANNON** *leaves.*)

ELEANOR. Have we had enough of this?

SARAH. Not yet.

ELEANOR. I am so tired, my love!

SARAH. Go to bed then.

ELEANOR. Will you come with me?

(**ELEANOR** *puts her head on* **SARAH***'s shoulder.*)

Have pity on a poor old hag.

SARAH. Oh, for goodness sake.

(*A moment of intimacy is broken by the entrance of* **MARY.***)

MARY CARYLL. The Duke of Wellington.

DUKE OF WELLINGTON. My dear ladies.

ELEANOR. My Lord.

(They sit for dinner.)

(Voices heard from off.)

CHARLES. Upon our meeting I was nearly convulsed. There is not one point to distinguish them from men: the dressing and powdering of the hair; their well-starched neck cloths. They looked exactly like two respectable superannuated old clergymen.

LADY STANLEY. I found them more unaffected and less clever than I expected ...but in their garden they were delightful, and seem to lead a most enviable and happy life.

CHARLES MATTHEWS. I longed to put Lady Eleanor under a bell-glass, and bring her to Highgate, for you to look at.

LONDSDALE. I think Lady Eleanor is very clever, very odd, and the greatest flatterer I ever met with. On the whole she was very entertaining, and appeared to have read a great deal.

NEWSPAPER JOURNALIST. Miss Ponsonby is polite and effeminate, fair and beautiful. She is of a calmer and more reserved disposition; there is a winning mildness in her manner, though a strange melancholy diffused over her person.

LONDSDALE. Miss Ponsonby only seems to assent to what Lady Eleanor says and speaks little herself.

HANMER. Lady Eleanor's manners are abrupt, and sharp. She is the most unwelcoming host.

*(**WORDSWORTH** enters, unseen by the ladies. Covered in mud and hay.)*

WORDSWORTH. Excuse me, a moment of assistance. It appears I am rather lost.

Would you happen to know where I may find the virgins of the bower?

MARY. Who?

WORDSWORTH. The Sisters of the Valley?

The Women of the Wild Welsh garden?

Those most highly regarded and mysterious madames of the mount?

Please, I'm really very cold and in need of shelter.

I've come from London.

MARY. What do you do then?

WORDSWORTH. I'm a poet.

MARY. Makes sense.

ELEANOR!

SARAH!

(**ELEANOR** *and* **SARAH** *hear* **MARY** *calling.*)

ELEANOR. When shall we be quite alone?

SARAH. Do you not want to have friends?

ELEANOR. Not really, no.

Thought that was sort of the point of all this.

SARAH. That was absolutely not the point.

Come on.

There's no time for this.

ELEANOR. There's never any time.

SARAH. Don't keep everyone waiting then.

Come in!

(MARY enters with WORDSWORTH.)

MARY. Found a wandering minstrel for you,

Starved of his supper.

Shall I wrap him up some innards?

SARAH. Ah, Mr Wordsworth.

(Dinner is eaten and then WORDSWORTH rises from the table.)

WORDSWORTH. A verse!

To the Lady Eleanor and the Honourable Miss Ponsonby

Composed in the grounds of Plas Newydd – Lan... Larn...

ELEANOR. Llangollen

WORDSWORTH. Yes.

A stream to mingle with your favourite Dee

Along the Vale of Meditation flows;

So styled by those fierce Britons, pleased to see

In Nature's face the expression of repose,

Or, haply there some pious Hermit chose

To live and die—the peace of Heaven his aim,

To whom the wild sequestered region owes

At this late day, its sanctifying name.

Glyn Cafaillgaroch, in the Cambrian tongue,

In ours the Vale of Friendship, let this spot

Be nam'd, where faithful to a low roof'd Cot

On Deva's banks, ye have abode so long,

Sisters in love, a love allowed to climb

Ev'n on this earth, above the reach of time.

(Silence follows.)

SARAH.   Thank you Mr Wordsworth, that was... remarkable.

WORDSWORTH. Just a small offer.

(Beat.)

SARAH. Sisters in love, yes?

WORDSWORTH. Yes.

SARAH. Of course, we are not sisters.

WORDSWORTH. No, of course.

SARAH. We are often muddled such.

WORDSWORTH. A mere turn of phrase.

SARAH. Sisters in Love...(S)sters... in love... perhaps lovers might have been more succinct?

WORDSWORTH. Well now, I hardly think that would be appropriate.

SARAH. No?

(Beat.)

WORDSWORTH. It's just the assonance, you see, Sissssters... Lovers would not work.

SARAH. I see.

(Beat.)

ELEANOR. Forgive us, my dear Sarah is quite the pedant for formalities, Mr Wordsworth. We are honoured, truly. Are we not?

SARAH. Oh no, indeed.

ELEANOR. Sarah is quite the poet herself.

WORDSWORTH. Oh, well good for you.

> (**MARY** *enters and hands* **WORDSWORTH** *a brownish liquid.*)

MARY. A recipe for a violent cough or anything nasty that affects the lungs. Take the four trotters of a sheep. They will need to be scalded so make sure you remove the hair. Split them in twain and mix with two quarts milk in an earthen pan. Cook for as long as dry bread. When cold, remove the feet and white skin with a small spoon.

Take a large mugful of broth each morning until recovered.

Add nutmeg for extra flavour.

> (**MARY** *exits.*)

WORDSWORTH. Actually, it is getting rather late in the day – I'd best call for a coach.

SARAH. Will you not stay for the garden, Sir?

WORDSWORTH. Perhaps tomorrow, the journey here was most rambunctious with all the potholes and muck, I fear my stomach will soon be most unwell. I shall take my leave.

> (**WORDSWORTH** *goes to take his hat and leave.*)

SARAH. Oh well I'm sure we could ask Mary to...

WORDSWORTH. *(On way out.)* Thank you SO much for a lovely evening.

> (*He is gone.* **SARAH** *follows him out and then turns back to* **ELEANOR.***)*

SARAH. Oh come on, he was asking for that.

ELEANOR. Disgraceful behaviour altogether.

SARAH. ME?!

> (**SARAH** *sits with her reading.* **ELEANOR**
> *watches her.*)

Sisters in love?

ELEANOR. I'm not getting into this.

SARAH. A love allowed to climb, oh well then, if it but
please you my Lord.

ELEANOR. Stop it, he may come back.

SARAH. I expect he's halfway to the Lake District by now
with news from the Vale of Friendship.

> (*Beat.*)

> (**SARAH** *sits at* **ELEANOR**'s *feet and reads her
> book.*)

ELEANOR. What are you reading?

SARAH. Voltaire.

ELEANOR. Didn't think we liked him.

SARAH. I do.

ELEANOR. Oh.

> (*Pause.*)

SARAH. "All I know," said Candide, "is that we must
cultivate our garden." – "You are right," said Pangloss,
"for when man was placed in the garden of Eden, he
was put there 'ut operaretur eum', so that he might
work: which proves that man was not born for the
rest."– Let us set to work, for that is the only way to
make life bearable.'

ELEANOR. That sounds bloody depressing.

(Beat.)

SARAH. Why are you so afraid of everyone who comes to see us?

They like us, I think.

They might not understand, but we are respected.

ELEANOR. They come here and they see only what they will.

What we let them.

Friends. Sisters. Wards of care. Middle-aged women dressed in mens' clothes growing mad in a garden.

They can see us, but they cannot know us.

If they really knew us they would be/

SARAH. What?

What would they be?

Shocked?

Appalled?

Disgusted?

ELEANOR. Probably far worse.

SARAH. So, you'd rather hide away in fear forever, would you?

(Beat.)

Sisters he called us.

Sisters.

Wanted to be sick.

Didn't you?

ELEANOR. Of course I did.

SARAH. But you didn't say anything. Why not?

ELEANOR. Sarah, I have only ever wanted to protect you from harm.

SARAH. I don't want your protection.

ELEANOR. What do you want then?

(Beat.)

*(***SARAH*** kisses ***ELEANOR.****)*

*(Momentarily ***ELEANOR*** lets her, and then ***SARAH*** tries to be more passionate with ***ELEANOR.****)*

Sarah, stop it.

SARAH. Don't you want me?

*(***SARAH*** tries to kiss ***ELEANOR*** again.)*

Please.

ELEANOR. Stop it Sarah.

*(***SARAH*** keeps trying to touch ***ELEANOR*** until finally ***ELEANOR*** pushes her away.)*

Sarah, stop it!!!

*(***ELEANOR*** pushes ***SARAH*** from her.)*

What the hell do you think you're doing?

SARAH. I just want to feel normal.

ELEANOR. And you think that was normal, do you?

Do you think all that is what normal people do?

SARAH. When they live as we do, yes.

(Beat.)

Do you love me?

ELEANOR. Enough of this.

SARAH. Do you?

ELEANOR. I think I've made my feelings abundantly clear by now, don't you?

SARAH. Say it then.

In words.

In your words.

ELEANOR. Why?

SARAH. Because words are important.

> (**ELEANOR** *tries to speak and finds she can't.*)

See, you can't. Can you?

You are ashamed.

ELEANOR. I'm not.

SARAH. It's me then, is it?

Are you ashamed of me?

ELEANOR. No.

SARAH. Why are you so afraid to love me?

ELEANOR. You really don't understand this, do you?

SARAH. Stop saying that to me.

I've had enough of that.

I am not your pupil anymore.

ELEANOR. There's no money left.

SARAH. What do you mean?

ELEANOR. The expenses for the grounds and the garden.

We've overspent by thousands.

We are entirely over our heads.

SARAH. But, your brother?

ELEANOR. He's cut me off. His wife said she could have no part in supporting a degenerate spinster. They've cut me out of everything. I've no lands, no title, no inheritance.

Everything we have here now rests on those people out there who believe what they are told.

I want you to think carefully about the story you want to tell them.

We know who we are.

Does it matter if we have to bend the truth little in order to not break it entirely?

Did we not come here to live in peace?

SARAH. No, actually. I don't think that's why I came at all.

ELEANOR. What did you come for then?

(**SARAH** *says nothing.*)

Well?

SARAH. I can't say that I know anymore.

(*Beat.*)

ELEANOR. Then why are you still here?

(**ELEANOR** *leaves.*)

(**MARY** *enters.*)

MARY. Miss Sarah, are you well?

(**SARAH** *cannot speak.*)

I'll call Lady Eleanor –

SARAH. No! No. Don't.

MARY. A letter for you.

(**MARY** *passes* **SARAH** *a letter.* **SARAH** *opens it.*)

SARAH. Where's the coachman?

MARY. Up to his beak in a pint I'd reckon, why?

Where are we –

SARAH. Shhhhh.

(**SARAH** *goes to leave.*)

MARY. Where are you going?

SARAH. Home.

MARY. But you are/

(**SARAH** *exits.*)

Ah, here.

(**ELEANOR** *enters.*)

ELEANOR. Sarah?

Sarah?

Where is she?

MARY. I/

ELEANOR. Have you seen this?

MARY. What?

(**ELEANOR** *throws down a newspaper article.*)

(*The headline is 'Extraordinary Female Affection'.*)

(**MARY** *picks up the article.*)

ELEANOR. We are ruined.

MARY. What does it say?

ELEANOR. A dangerous pack of lies.

MARY. Is it?

Where?

ELEANOR. Can't you read?

(**ELEANOR** *snatches the paper back.*)

Extraordinary Female Affection – A comprehensive study into the romantic friendship of the Ladies of Llangollen.

(**MARY** *tries to hold the paper in the light so she can read.*)

It's everywhere.

We have to leave.

MARY. Why?

ELEANOR. We are not safe here.

MARY. There is nobody here but me.

ELEANOR. Yes, and it's people like you that got us into this mess, isn't it? Why can't you people keep your bloody mouths shut?

(**ELEANOR** *starts packing up papers to leave.*)

No more of this.

I am going to sort this out.

Don't speak to anyone.

Don't let any of them –

You stay here.

(**ELEANOR** *runs out.*)

Scene Four

Holyhead Port

footnote

(*We follow* **SARAH** *through music and movement back through to Holyhead port, where she stands alone watching the boats boarding back to Ireland.*)

(**LADY BETTY***'s voice is heard.*)

LADY BETTY. My Dearest child.

I write to you once and once only. I had thought there would be more time to right the wrongs that have befallen us, but soon I fear I shall not have the strength to even dictate this letter to my Dear Mrs Goddard, who is come to sit with me and ensure I am not alone at the very end.

My time on this earth is slipping away from me now, quicker than I imagined, but not fast enough to spare me the loss of Dear Sir William, who left us just a few short weeks ago. His end, like the last years of his life, was painful, rageful and full of deepest woe. Sir William was a man most afraid of himself. I hope when we are soon reunited his soul shall have found peace, as he was good in his heart - and I do believe he loved us both deeply.

My Sarah - the greatest grief and sorrow I have in this world is parting with you and the thoughts of your sorrow for me.

Don't grieve for me, I am, trust in God, going to be happy. You have my sincere prayers and thanks for your tenderness to me and good behaviour. If I ever offended you forgive me. I have never meant any offence, I have only ever meant to be a good wife and Mother and I hope you still think of me so.

Nobody to be at my funeral except my own poor, who I think should be sorry for me.

Take care of yourself (live and do all as good as you can) and may God almighty give you a peaceful and happy ending.

God grant you happiness in all that you do and all that you are.

Your Lady Betty.

> (**SARAH** *stands with the letter at the port.*)

> (*Suddenly* **MARY** *runs in, totally out of breath.*)

MARY. Stop. Stop right where you are. For the love of God to not take another step or you'll have murder on your soul.

SARAH. What are you doing here?

MARY. What am I ... Oh, would you listen to it!

Just fancied a nice stroll, watch the boats go by.

Nice bit of exercise, good for the old heart, you know.

SARAH. Did you follow me?

MARY. You've the whole place up in arms.

Seriously, could the pair of you not at least give a bit of notice before you do your little disappearing act?

I'm fifteen years older than last time, you know.

I can't keep up.

SARAH. Where's Eleanor?

MARY. Never mind her, we'll get to that later.

I've only got these two legs, you see.

> (**MARY** *sits down to get her breath back.*)

Going on another little adventure then, were we?!

(**SARAH** *does not answer.*)

Where were we headed this time?

SARAH. That boat sets sail for Waterford.

MARY. Long journey that.

Had you thought to pack a sandwich?

Clean socks?

And I assume you've remembered your fare for the boatman there.

SARAH. I/

MARY. Ah, Jaysus, the absolute state of ye.

Money is wasted on the rich, it really us.

Are you hungry?

SARAH. A bit.

(**MARY** *throws* **SARAH** *a large raw vegetable.*)

MARY. Now.

What are you doing here?

SARAH. Sir William is dead.

MARY. God rest him.

SARAH. Lady Betty is soon to follow him.

She wrote to me.

MARY. Did she ask you to come?

SARAH. No.

MARY. Then you've still not answered my question.

(*Beat.*)

SARAH. I gave up everything for this.

Was it worth it, do you think?!

All this... fighting.

Fighting to be seen, fighting not to be seen, fighting for her, and for what?

Where's it left me?

I'm still on my own here, aren't I?

MARY. Are you now?

> (**MARY** *offers some more food from her apron for comfort, which she takes.*)

SARAH. What would you do now, if you were me?

MARY. Nobody cares about that.

This is your story.

You chose what to do with it.

SARAH. What if I make a bad choice?

MARY. Choose again then.

You're lucky you.

All these choices.

Waste to only try one, if you ask me.

> (*Beat.*)

Now, if you don't mind – I am going to go over there to administer myself into that small hedge and let nature take its course.

If there's one thing you can quote me on let it be this – I do not travel well.

> (**MARY** *goes to leave.*)

SARAH. What did you come here for?

*(**MARY** looks back.)*

MARY. Me?!

I'm just here for the clean up, am I not?

SARAH. You're not though, are you?!

(Beat.)

MARY. For love then.

I'm here for love.

SARAH. What... do you have a/

MARY. There is more than one kind.

SARAH. And that's enough for you?

MARY. That has been enough for me, yes.

But it's not my story, is it?

*(**MARY** exits and leaves **SARAH** alone with the letter.)*

Scene Five

A Lawyer's Office

(An elderly gentleman, **EDMUND BURKE** *is sitting working at his desk.)*

(Lights up as **ELEANOR** *enters and stands in front of him.)*

EDMUND. May the Gods be gentle, is it Lady Eleanor Butler that stands before me?

ELEANOR. Edmund, I am here to beg of you swift and fierce retribution on those who have come to cause me harm.

To the full extent of your capabilities.

> *(**EDMUND** signals to one of the witnesses.)*

EDMUND. Tea, we must have tea.

Urgently.

All the sugar you can stuff in it.

> *(The witness goes to make tea.)*

> *(**EDMUND** goes back to **ELEANOR** and then calls after him.)*

And crack open the millefeuille!

Now.

Would you like to sit down?

> *(**ELEANOR** bursts into tears as **EDMUND** sits her down.)*

ELEANOR. I'm so sorry Edmund.

EDMUND. It's perfectly alright dear, I'm a lawyer.

That chair's seen a lot worse, I assure you.

Here.

> *(He gives her his handkerchief.)*

I was told in training to always keep one spare.

> *(Witness comes in with tea and millefeuille, cut in slices.)*

Thank you, kindly.

> *(**SIR EDMUND** pours the tea.)*

Now.

Is there any truth in these frightful rumours I have heard?!

ELEANOR. I/

SIR WILLIAM. Forty two breeds of roses?!

ELEANOR. There's forty three now.

The last bloomed only this week.

EDMUND. Heaven bless me.

You mustn't have me stay, you know.

I fear I should simply burst in joyous rapture upon arrival and cause you all a great inconvenience.

> *(**ELEANOR** laughs.)*

ELEANOR. It is very beautiful.

EDMUND. I should say so indeed.

Cake?

> *(**EDMUND** offers her the cake.)*

This is about the article, of course.

ELEANOR. You've read it?!

EDMUND. Oh, God no.

I wouldn't lower myself to open that drivel.

I've a friend in High Wycombe who passes by here on occasion, works for the Irish consulate.

They were sent a copy in the morning report.

Everyone's up in arms about it.

Calling for a full boycott on the General Post.

ELEANOR. Really?

EDMUND. Well, of course.

Especially with all the good you pair are doing them all for Anglo-Irish trading relations.

You must know that there is a report sent there often from Llangollen council of the impact of your charitable donations to the poor townsfolk?

ELEANOR. No, I didn't know that.

EDMUND. Do you not hear it from the locals?

ELEANOR. We don't really go out very often.

EDMUND. Perhaps you should.

ELEANOR. Where on earth has this story come from then?

EDMUND. The fiery chasms of a very bitter little man's very uneventful marital bed, I'd wager.

Nasty little rattlesnakes, those writers.

ELEANOR. What can we do about it?

EDMUND. What do you want me to do?

ELEANOR. Can we sue?

EDMUND. For what?

ELEANOR. Libel?

EDMUND. Well, what have they written?

ELEANOR. Terrible things!

EDMUND. That is not in dispute dear, but what have they written?

ELEANOR. Here.

> (**ELEANOR** *gives him the article.*)

> (*He puts on his spectacles and reads it.*)

EDMUND. Oh dear.

Dear, dear me.

Savages.

> (*He puts the paper down.*)

Lady Eleanor I need read no more, my time here is too precious.

You have my word that first thing tomorrow morning there shall be a headed letter of disdain to greet them, written with the bluntest, most poisonous end of my quill.

ELEANOR. What about prosecution?

EDMUND. Well now, that depends.

Come now, sit here.

> (**EDMUND** *sits her at the desk.*)

> (*He hands her a pen and a magnifying glass.*)

You read that again, and carefully.

Circle anything in that article that is an untruth.

Anything at all.

If you can provide me with evidence of even the smallest of misinformations about yourself or your good Lady, we can unmask the cannons and unleash merry hell.

> (**ELEANOR** *reads the article again. A few times she gasps as if she has found something, and then realises that it isn't actually untrue, and keeps reading.*)

ELEANOR. I have it! I have it!

EDMUND. Go on!

ELEANOR. I'm NOT tall!

EDMUND. I'm not sure even I can get that one past the prosecution.

Anything else?

> (**ELEANOR** *keeps looking then throws the article away from her.*)

ELEANOR. This is TOTAL HORESHIT!

EDMUND. Yes it is rather, isn't it?

Are you sure you wouldn't like some millefeuille, it's quite the rage in the tea rooms this season.

> (**ELEANOR** *grabs a piece of millefeuille and shoves it into her face, angrily.*)

Lady Eleanor, please forgive me, I fear I am not providing you with the solutions you hoped for today.

ELEANOR. Could we not just give it a go anyway?

They've thrown me under the wheels like a bloody lame horse.

EDMUND. Yes well we certainly could give it a try, but I fear in doing so I may end up doing you a great disservice.

ELEANOR. How so?

EDMUND. Well because in a court of law, the only thing a half decent lawyer aims to prove is the cold hard truth.

And our truth my dear, if they get their greasy hands on it, is one that many would like to see thrown on the woodpile and burned to ashes - and us along with it.

But that doesn't mean we have to let them, does it?

It just means we must keep it safe.

ELEANOR. Yes, only I'm not sure that does keep it safe really Edmund, does it?

If we have to constantly hide ourselves from view, I'm not sure that anyone will ever be able to prove that we ever even existed at all.

And where does that leave us?

EDMUND. Interesting gambit, you'd have done well in law you know.

Take heart, my dear.

Your consolation must be that you suffer along with everything that is excellent in the world.

Now, if you'll excuse me, my curfew hour is fast approaching.

I must soon be home to my wife.

She does worry if I am not home for supper call and I like to save my precious few late cards for more pressing appointments with the fair gentleman of the Irish consulate.

Before I take my leave, I must ask -

This new rose, has it a name?

ELEANOR. Rosa Mundi.

EDMUND. Rosa Mundi.

And what does it mean?

ELEANOR. The Rose of the World.

EDMUND. Yes that's it. Beautiful.

Go back to your garden, Eleanor.

Stay with what is beautiful.

(**EDMUND BURKE** *exits.*)

(**SARAH** *and* **ELEANOR** *travel back to Plas Newydd.*)

Scene Six

Plas Newydd, Llangollen

(SARAH enters. ELEANOR is sitting at her desk. They remain in silence for a while. Then;.)

ELEANOR. Why did you come back?

SARAH. For love.

I'm here for love.

What about you?

(SARAH goes to move towards ELEANOR and she stops her.)

ELEANOR. I had a maid once.

Victoria.

She came to us to look after my brother but he wouldn't be placed with a woman, and they'd agreed to her board for six months so she was passed over to me.

I'd never had my own maid before. People came and went all the time, and they did things for me, they did everything for me really, but they never noticed me. Not really. Sometimes I wondered if anybody saw me at all. I remember one of them looking me right in the face once when they were getting me dressed and honestly, it was like they saw nothing there but a crack in the wall.

Victoria listened.

Noticed when I did things.

Told me I was kind.

Sometimes, before bed, if she had no other chores, she would come into my room and read to me.

La Vie De Marianne.

She held me.

Nobody held me.

One night, my Father came home and asked to have dinner with me.

He never, ever did that.

So I went down and I sat opposite him, great big long glass table, just me and him.

He asked me about Victoria.

And I remember I was scared to tell him at first because I honestly don't think he'd ever asked me a question before... but then I started speaking about her a bit and I found I couldn't stop.

I told him how kind she was. How much happier I felt when she was near me. How warm and soft and gentle she was. I spoke about her for a really long time, and he didn't interrupt. He listened very carefully to every word I said. I think it's probably the longest I ever spoke to him for.

When I'd finished speaking he said nothing, he just got up and left.

The next day she was gone.

We never saw her again.

I don't know what happened to her.

I just know that they took her away.

Because I loved her.

And when I spoke,

When I gave them my words, they took them from me.

And they were lost.

I don't want to be lost anymore.

>	*(Beat.)*

My name is Eleanor Butler.

I am the first daughter of Kilkenny castle.

And I love you, Sarah Ponsonby.

That is the truest thing.

The most beautiful thing.

Those are the only words that matter.

Could that be enough?

SARAH. Enough for me.

>	*(**SARAH** takes **ELEANOR***'s hand.)*

>	*(**ELEANOR** kisses **SARAH** passionately.)*

ELEANOR. Now.

Scene Seven

Plas Newydd, Llangollen

(More diary entries. Showing the passing of time, the days spent together, the changing of the seasons.)

ELEANOR. September 29th – The Barrets and Miss Davies came at twelve. They left at four. When they were gone my beloved and I walked our garden, and then sat by the fire together till ten.

SARAH. October 30th – Sweet and delicate day. We went to our bank – planted all the cowslips – primroses – violets – lily of the valley.

ELEANOR. November 5th – My beloved and I walked through the white gate. The finest night sky – constellations – stars – planets – mists rising and gradually ascending the mountains from the rivers, brooks and streams. One large bonfire on the green. Bells ringing in commemoration of the revolution.

SARAH. December 22nd – Rose at eight after a tedious night spent coughing with the most dreadful headache. My dearest, my kindest love did not sleep for one moment the entire night but lay beside me watching and lamenting my illness, soothing by her tenderness the distressing pain in my head.

ELEANOR. January 7th – From two till three we read Tableau de la suisse. My beloved at her maps. Spent the evening without candles, by the light of the fire and faint glimmering of the pale moon, talking over our affairs. My sweet love. A silent, pensive day.

(The ladies leave.)

*(**MARY** comes back.)*

MARY. Has anyone got a quill and ink?

> *(She looks around the audience.)*

Feckin' useless.

> *(She calls down a witness.)*

You there.

Yes you

WITNESS. Yes, Miss.

MARY. Write this down.

> *(The **WITNESS** goes to get a quill and ink.)*

I, Mary Caryll ...

Mary looks around to find the witness running back.

Are you listening now?

> *(**WITNESS** nods.)*

I, Mary Caryll, being of reasonably sound mind and body - bequeath all my earthly possessions and belongings to my dearest friend, Miss Sarah Ponsonby. Included in this are the following: my dearest cat Muff, that she may live safe from the violent hands of Farmer Morgan, the field given to me by the Ladies to grow my potatoes, and my entire life savings, accrued over the years from the kind tips of visitors, which you shall find stored safely in a hessian sack under my bed.

It is my expressed desire that this money should be used to clear any debts accrued by their less than prudent spending, and that they should use the remaining funds to achieve a mortgage on Plas Newydd, Llangollen - and live there in peace without unwanted disturbance for the rest of their days.

Did you hear me ?

WITNESS. Yes.

MARY. Am I understood?

WITNESS. You are.

MARY. Good.

Now.

(**MARY** *Exits.*)

Scene Eight

Plas Newydd, Llangollen

*(We watch aged **ELEANOR** and **SARAH** walk around their garden, for a little while.)*

(Then they sit.)

*(**SARAH** starts sticking up **ELEANOR**'s hair with loads of white powder.)*

SARAH. Do we have to do this every time?

ELEANOR. Absolutely.

SARAH. You gave the choristers an awful fright last week.

ELEANOR. Did I?

SARAH. Yes, they thought they'd seen a ghoul.

ELEANOR. HA! That'll teach them for spying on me.

*(**SARAH** places a large, gaudy purple cross around **ELEANOR**'s neck.)*

How is it looking?

SARAH. Terribly unfashionable.

ELEANOR. Marvellous.

SARAH. We will be stared at, you know.

ELEANOR. One of the great benefits of losing one's sight.

They can stare as much as they like.

*(**ELEANOR** feels the cross.)*

We'll have some more of those I think.

One for each season.

*(**SARAH** finishes **ELEANOR**'s hair.)*

SARAH. Now.

ELEANOR. How do I look?

SARAH. Stunning.

(**SARAH** *kisses* **ELEANOR.**)

ELEANOR. Have we found the words?

SARAH. I think so.

ELEANOR. Read it to me then.

SARAH. Right.

(**SARAH** *gets a bit of paper out.*)

Released from Earth and all its transient woes,

She whose remains beneath this stone repose,

Steadfast in Faith resigned her parting breath,

Looked up with Christian joy and smiled in Death!

Patient, Industrious, Faithful, Generous, Kind,

Her Conduct left the proudest far behind,

Her Virtues dignified her humble birth,

And raised her mind about this sordid earth.

Attachment (Sacred bond of grateful breasts)

Extinguished but with life, this Tomb attests,

Reared by Two Friends who will her loss bemoan,

Till with Her Ashes... Here shall rest, Their own.

ELEANOR. The ending's a bit ominous.

SARAH. Shall I change it?

ELEANOR. No, no it's good. Morbid. She'd like that.

(**ELEANOR** *holds* **SARAH** *gently.*)

SARAH. What are we going to do now?

ELEANOR. Carry on.

That tends to be the way of it.

SARAH. Do you know, I was sat the other day with the priest and he asked me about her family – and I realised I had no idea who they were. Do you?

ELEANOR. Never thought she had any.

SARAH. Of course she did.

ELEANOR. She never mentioned them.

SARAH. I can't just say she didn't have any, can I?

ELEANOR. Put us down then.

SARAH. We weren't family.

ELEANOR. Close enough, wouldn't you say?

(Beat.)

SARAH. I wish she hadn't been on her own.

ELEANOR. Her end was as she wanted it.

Can't ask for better than that.

(Beat.)

We must keep each other very close from now on.

*(**SARAH** looks at **ELEANOR** for a moment in the mirror.)*

SARAH. Do you like this part?

ELEANOR. It is my favourite, actually.

Two musty old bats.

SARAH. Mad women on the hill.

ELEANOR. If we come back and do this again, shall we start as old women?

SARAH. Story would be very short.

ELEANOR. Doesn't have to be.

Depends on where we end it.

Now?

Scene Nine

Plas Newydd, Llangollen

*(The ladies dance together in their garden,
free from all burdens.)*

EDMUND BURKE. It is impossible to describe the feelings
of the inhabitants of Llangollen, as we today mourn the
loss of our own Lady Eleanor Butler, who is departed
from us at the age of ninety.

All who can afford it are in deepest mourning, and the
poorer of the town to whom she was the most loyal
benefactor weep and bewail the loss of her.

Her funeral is of royal standing – her coffin supported
by twelve bearers, four clergymen, two physicians
and three surgeons. All shops closed, businesses at a
standstill and as the grand procession passed by, barely
a dry eye in the town was to be seen.

Lady Eleanor's dearest friend, Miss Sarah Ponsonby,
with whom she had lived in romantic friendship for
over fifty one years – was not in attendance.

Scene Ten

Modern Day, Plas Newydd, Llangollen

(Guests in modern dress come to take a tour in Plas Newydd.)

*(**SARAH** enters, she watches them, holding a flower.)*

(The flower is real and alive.)

SARAH. Do you understand us now ?

Do you see us now?

Do you hear us now?

Do you know us now?

And so, what happens next here?

Shall we be free?

Shall we live?

Shall we be quite alone?

> *(**ELEANOR** arrives, dressed as she would be today.)*

> *(She takes **SARAH** by the hand.)*

ELEANOR. Now.

> *(They watch the people in their house and in the audience, hearing their story. Then they leave, together.)*

End

Lightning Source UK Ltd.
Milton Keynes UK
UKHW020850150522
403003UK00001B/3